"What a deeply valuable book Lesley Hazleton has written. Sadly, many people have been misled, if not deceived, by the facile, often thoughtless ways psychological issues are presented to the public. But here is a book that is sure, wise, and reassuring. It honors people as well as a complex and often vexing discipline. Funny how the 'non-how-to' books typically offer the best counsel."

Thomas J. Cottle
Harvard Medical School

"Lesley Hazleton's book is powerful, persuasive and brave. Its readers may continue feeling depressed every now and then, but they will no longer feel depressed about their depression."

Letty Cottin Pogrebin
Author of *Family Politics* and
Growing up Free

"Lesley Hazleton is fierce, bright, witty and wise. She has written a guidebook to the blues which turns out to be, in part, a handbook to happiness and, in part, an accessible and moving text on the everyday unsolvable problems of our emotional lives."

Maureen Howard

"Humane and reassuring writing on the pursuit of happiness and the darker days along the way."
Publishers Weekly

The Right to

Feel Bad

Coming to Terms with Normal Depression

Lesley Hazleton

BALLANTINE BOOKS • NEW YORK

Lines from "Crude Foyer" Copyright © 1947 by Wallace Stevens, from *The Collected Poems of Wallace Stevens.* Reprinted by permission of Alfred A. Knopf, Inc.
"Resumé" Copyright © 1926, renewed © 1954 by Dorothy Parker, from *The Portable Dorothy Parker.* Reprinted by permission of Viking/Penguin, Inc.
From "Monotony" in *The Complete Poems of Cavafy,* translated and copyright © 1961 by Rae Dalven. Reprinted by permission of Harcourt Brace Jovanovich, Inc.
From *The Cocktail Party,* copyright 1950 by T. S. Eliot; renewed 1978 by Esme Valerie Eliot. Reprinted by permission of Harcourt Brace Jovanovich, Inc.

Library of Congress Catalog Card Number: 83-20627

ISBN 0-345-32401-3

This edition published by arrangement with The Dial Press

Manufactured in the United States of America

First Ballantine Books Edition: July 1985

Acknowledgments

Without the hundreds of people who found the time and the courage to talk to me about their depressions, this book would never have been possible. *In order to protect the privacy of those whom I have quoted directly, I have used fictionalized names instead of their real names.*

My deepest thanks are also due to the many psychologists, psychiatrists and analysts with whom I discussed this book and who supported it in various ways. I am particularly indebted to the writings of Ernest Becker, which helped shape much of my basic thinking in this book.

Especial thanks are due to two people—to my editor, Joyce Johnson, for her gentle ruthlessness, and to my agent, Gloria Loomis, for her unwavering encouragement and support. Thanks also to the MacDowell Colony, for the tranquility in which to write, and to the New York Public Library for use of the Wertheim and Allen research rooms.

Contents

1 *The Right to Feel Bad*

All of us know those bad times. There seems to be no point in getting out of bed. In fact there seems to be no point in anything at all. All sense of purpose is lost. "Why should I get up? Why go to work? What's the use of it?" we might ask. And only silence reverberates in answer.

All sense of warmth in life seems to have fled. The sun may be shining, the sky may be blue, but so far as we are concerned, there is only a monotonous slate gray reaching to the far horizons of our lives. The gray pervades everything, draining all color from things we usually cherish. We feel empty; the world feels empty. We have no faith left in ourselves or in the world. At that point, we might even wonder, "What is the point of living at all?"

Or it may simply be that the thousand small struggles of daily life just suddenly become too much. We find ourselves asking, "Why am I doing this?"—and again we find no answer.

Perhaps the worst of such times is when there seems to be no immediate reason for such thoughts and questions. Everything may be going well enough, not wonderfully but then not so terribly either, and yet . . . Something seems to be missing, something so impalpable we can't say what it is, but so vital that it drains everything else of meaning. We feel just plain miserable and are frightened by how we feel since no solid reason presents itself to comfort us with a clear pattern of cause and effect. All that exists is depression.

Nearly everyone gets depressed. That basic feeling of emptiness, exhaustion, and meaninglessness is universal, crossing all borders of age, sex, and nationality. Winston Churchill called it his "black dog," always waiting to bare its teeth at him. Psychiatrists say it is "the common cold" of their profession. A systems analyst thinks of it as a "stinky old blanket" that she carries around with her. But whatever image each of us has created for the depression we occasionally experience, we carry the burden of it with shame and guilt. After all, we are not "meant" to feel this way. All depression, we have been convinced, is either sick or wrong.

We are haunted by the constantly reiterated fact that between five and fifteen percent of the population suffer from severe depression. This is so. But then what about the rest of us, the vast majority of us? We too get depressed. We suffer through it for hours, days, and even weeks at a time, but emerge from it by ourselves, without psychiatric aid. How are we to see our depression? How are we to struggle through those difficult and painful times without berating ourselves for the very fact of being depressed? How are we to deal with feeling bad when the world around us seems to insist on only feeling good?

Hiding our depression out of fear and shame lest others see it, we do not realize that everyone has experienced the same thing. Even those we might think never give way to depression turn out to be well acquainted with it, as I found to my amazement when I first began work on this book.

A friend whom I had thought had never been depressed in his life declared himself "a long-time expert on the subject," and then turned the tables on me by asking why I should want to write about it.

"But isn't that obvious?" I replied, parrying question with question in my surprise. "I also get depressed."

"You?" he answered, clearly astonished. And I was suddenly aware of how expert I had become at subterfuge—at how expert all of us have had to become. Inside we may feel as though we and the world were breaking apart, but we continue "as though" —as though everything were just fine and we had never heard of the word "depression." And though we may be able to deceive everyone else, we do not deceive ourselves.

Still, we do everything we can to avoid the questions depression forces upon us. Even to ask "What is the point?" challenges everything we usually take for granted, so we avert our eyes if we can, try to get down under the blankets of life, or attempt to drown out the questions in drink or work or hectic activity. Those of us who cannot manage this, ask the questions in fear and trembling, with silent screams so loud that there is no quiet space in which to sit and calmly face them.

Indeed, we have become so terrified of our own depression that we refuse to face it. It has been made into a fearful void, a vast region of danger that we must avoid at any price, lest it cost us our self-respect, even our lives. In our terror, we have made an ogre out of a normal emotion.

The ogre's counterpart, the knight in shining armor, is meant to be happiness, riding in to rescue us. And indeed it is natural enough to want to feel good. Who in their right minds would not want to be loved, respected, secure, contented, and happy? But when we are told that this is the *only* way we should feel, and that everything else is wrong, the pursuit of happiness becomes a desperate matter, catching us in a viselike clutch.

Feeling good is no longer simply a right, but a social and personal duty. We have become convinced that if we do not feel good, we are at fault—weak or ill, dysfunctional or wrong. The right to feel good has been exaggerated out of all proportion—to the extent that we now have to reclaim the right to feel bad.

We have to reclaim the right to the whole range of feeling, including the right to mourn the vast range of loss that we are prey to. This is the right to react as human beings instead of as automatons who keep to the one path of happiness with grim determination, ignoring the realities of their lives.

We have to reject the artificial demand for a con-

stant high in life, and regain patience with the trials
and tribulations of living, with the natural rhythms
of ups and downs that give life a dynamic sense of
flow, movement, and change.

Common sense tells us that promises of "the key to
eternal happiness" are false, as tempting as the mi-
rage of water in the desert. Privately we acknowledge the fact that we do get depressed and struggle
with it as best we can. But what we feel clashes with
what we are constantly being told by the media and
by popular psychology, which have concentrated almost exclusively on severe depression.

Only a small part of depression is severe; most depression is normal. Since nearly all of us have experienced it at one time or another, how could we call it
anything else? And since it *is* a normal experience,
we must then begin to ask what function it fulfills.
Why do we get depressed? And what role does it play
in our lives?

The time for these questions is long overdue. We
need a fresh look at the whole subject, at the vast
range of depression as most of us know it. How are
we to see depression as a legitimate emotion? How
are we to avoid calling ourselves sick or wrong when
we feel it? How are we to reclaim it from the clutches
of those who claim that anything but feeling good is
bad?

This book is an attempt to answer these questions.
Like everyone who reads it, I too have a personal interest in it beyond authorship. For a long time I
thought that I was singularly cursed with depression. It terrified me and made me feel horribly isolated. In the lack of any concept of normal depression, I

thought that if I was depressed at all, I must be counted among that five to fifteen percent who are severely depressed.

True, each time I experienced it, it passed by itself. But knowing that was no help at all; each time anew I was convinced that it would never pass. At such times I seemed to exist in a hopeless void of emptiness and meaninglessness.

My suspicion that there was something seriously wrong with me was reinforced by the fact that I had occasionally flirted with the idea of suicide. I was never seriously close to the act itself, but the very fact of contemplating it made me feel "sick." I was not meant to think in such terms, I thought, nor meant to have such fantasies.

In the bright light of retrospect, of course, I can now argue that I should have known better. After all, I was a trained psychologist. I had been through psychoanalysis and even considered training as an analyst myself. But then psychological knowledge is notoriously frail when applied to oneself.

Sometimes these depressions would last a few days. There were longer bouts too—a week or two perhaps. And then came the bad ones—the time when for over a month I looked inside myself and found only emptiness.

I am not sure what else I could have expected at the time. I had just finished writing a book and was unsure if I wanted to return to regular journalism, a long-term relationship had been ended, and I had moved to New York. The major elements that had rooted me in life and given me a sense of belonging had gone. But they had gone by my own doing. I had chosen in each instance. Why then was I depressed?

Resentment invaded me. Couples walking arm in arm in the street reminded me of the love I had lost. The comfortable homes of friends reminded me of my homelessness. The intent purposefulness of rush hour crowds reminded me that I had no work I wanted to rush to. I was overwhelmed by a sense that all this was just no fair, that I deserved as good as any of these people around me—and even, in my nastier moments, that they deserved as bad as I.

I spent hours at a time sitting on the floor of my dingy sublet apartment, gazing out the window at a gray sky. "The world really *is* gray," I kept thinking. I slept a lot and woke up tired. I was exhausted and couldn't find the energy to do anything about it.

But after a month of this I could stand it no longer. I was angry and ashamed and disgusted at myself. Something had to break. And somewhere, unacknowledged, there was the determination that it would not be me.

Late one night, I was in that peculiar state of restlessness that precludes sleep even though sleep is all you want. It had begun to snow, and a bitter wind was howling around the corners of the building. I'm not sure why, but I threw on a coat and went out. There was some vague idea that if I could just walk far enough, I could make myself tired enough to sleep.

I headed right into the wind. Every now and then a car drove slowly up the avenue, leaving swerving tracks in the snow. Nobody else was on the sidewalks. The driving snow made my eyes water; the bitter cold seemed to blow right through my head. Yet there was something almost satisfying in it: the worst weather had been given me to tune in with my worst mood. And I slowly began to feel something other than misery. Even the weather was with me! I was not so alone after all! And from that thought, as I stood hunched up against the snow and the wind, it occurred to me that if I could write down how I felt, I might even be able to write it out of me. I turned, went home, and wrote all night and into the morning, then went to bed and slept the first really restful sleep in weeks.

Some months later I read through those impassioned notes for the first time. I began to trace what I could not see at the time—the pattern and the logic behind my depression. Tentatively, since the subject was still shameful, I began to talk to others about it, and that was the first time that I realized I was not alone, that almost everybody knew those same feelings firsthand. That realization determined me to write this book.

There followed nearly three years of questioning, reading, interviewing, and writing. During that time a very different perspective on depression emerged.

Chapters 2–4 of this book look at what has been done to depression—the numerous ways in which it has been stigmatized and invalidated, and the vast number of ways in which we have been persuaded that to feel bad at all is unacceptable. This means looking at the social and psychiatric pressures which have tried to determine how we *should* feel while ignoring the yawning gap between their "shoulds" and our reality.

Chapters 5–8 take a close look at the experience of depression itself, at what really happens in depression and why. This means exploring it not as an illness or malfunction, but as a healthy reaction to various kinds of loss and to the very real problem of existing in a complex and difficult world. Depression can then be seen not as a waste of time, but as a valuable process in which we think about the terms on which we exist, reexamine our values and our selves, and find the way to a renewed sense of purpose and meaning. Without such times, we would be the lesser people.

Chapters 9–11 explore ways in which we can come to terms with depression—accepting it, tolerating it, facing it without fear, and thus giving it a chance to fulfill its role in our lives. No magic pill will do the work for us. The new antidepressant drugs, though effective in severe depression, are of questionable use in normal depression. And though other drugs can be used to escape awareness, they also limit us as human beings.

To be fully alive means to experience the full range of emotions, to struggle with the downs as well as to enjoy the ups. Life is certainly difficult and even unpredictable—full of meaning and purpose at one time and utterly meaningless and purposeless at another; sometimes so desirable that we wish to freeze it at a certain point and remain there forever, and at other times so undesirable that we may find ourselves wishing we had never been born. But it also has its own dynamic. There is no real happiness without the experience of depression to balance it. If we are not capable of depression, we are not capable of happiness either. In a very real sense, depression keeps us alive.

Instead of fleeing it, then, we need to shed our shame and terror and see depression for what it is— not an ogre or enemy, but an integral part of life itself.

This book is thus basically a defense of depression. It takes a very different view from the one we have become accustomed to. Some have called it a kinder perspective. Others say it gives solace. I think of it simply as closer to what we all experience.

2 *The Happy Ideal*

> . . . we sit and breathe
> An innocence of an absolute,
> False happiness . . .
>
> WALLACE STEVENS

It had been some time since David and I had last seen each other. We had been lovers once, had remained close friends, and as friends had been through many adventures together—had been lost in the desert, had gone through wars, had talked passionately late into the night about ideas and events. It was a joy to see him again. Again we sat up late, talking, catching up so quickly on what we had been doing that soon it seemed as though we had last seen each other only yesterday. And then came the question:

"But, Lesley, are you happy?"

And suddenly I was not.

It must be one of the worst things that anyone can ask. You can be completely caught up in the spirit of what you are doing, and then that question stops you dead, held up at verbal gunpoint. "*Am* I happy?" you think. And as the mind races, trying to figure out if you are "really" happy, happiness vanishes like a gazelle surprised in the wild.

That time, I was pulled out of my pleasure at seeing David again by his sudden demand that I account for my life over the past two years in terms of happiness. They had been two years of struggle: not happy years, even in retrospect, but probably necessary ones. Happiness was a false measure to apply to that time—a demand that I justify it in terms of emotion rather than meaning.

Certainly there had been moments of happiness, well remembered, and longer moments of misery, not so well remembered, and then far longer times when I had been too busy to be aware of either.

And yet . . . Reason was one thing, feeling another. I longed to be able to answer David with a definite "yes." And since I could not do so, wondered where I had gone wrong.

Elusive and fleeting though we know it to be, we all still search for happiness, judging ourselves by whether we find it. What began as *a* right in the sense of entitlement—the right to the pursuit of happiness guaranteed in the American Declaration of Independence—has segued slowly into the sense of *being* right. Instead of a fortuitous sense of being, happiness has become a moral imperative.

This imposition of moral judgment on a state of being has even worked its way into the language. Many people describe depression, for instance, as "when I don't feel right" or "when I don't feel myself," as though the only self that is valid is the happy self. By now, happiness is feeling literally all right, and depression all wrong.

A system of "shoulds" has been constructed around the idea itself, inevitably creating guilt. The birth of a child, for example, should make the parents happy. It seems a sine qua non of life that this be so. Yet postpartum depression is a common reality, in fathers as well as mothers. A new job at better pay should make an ambitious young executive happy, yet a few weeks into the job the new employee may experience depression for what seems to be "no good reason." In both instances, the guilt over how they feel is as hard to bear as the depression itself.

The insistence on happiness can place sometimes intolerable strains on ordinary people. Constantly set up as the desired norm, it becomes oppressive. A young health worker attributes his depressions directly to the demand that he be happy. His parents wanted—as all parents do— only what was best for him. "I remember how in sixth grade, I was a good student, and my parents said to me: 'We don't mind what you want to be, a road cleaner or a scientist, an artist or a businessman. We just want you to know that we'll love you whatever you do, so long as you're happy.' And the implied message seemed obvious—if I wasn't happy, then they wouldn't love me anymore. And *that* made me unhappy! Since then whenever I get depressed, it seems to be at a time when I haven't been happy when I should have been."

Expecting happiness, we often make it impossible.

Determined to be happy, we make ourselves un-happy.

Yet as far as we can, we try to plan for happiness. In those two years since I had last seen David, for in-stance, I had traveled a lot in my work as a journal-ist. Surely this should have made me happy? After all, travel is presented by a consumer society as a major contributor to happiness, redolent of good times and carefree spending. I had been the envy of friends whose jobs held them in offices. Yet the real-ity was not quite their image of it.

Each time I was to leave for another country, an-other long trip, I felt an increasing unwillingness to move as the departure date neared. It was hard to ad-mit, even to myself: the admission gave the lie to the accepted image of the ideal life.

This desire to stay put stemmed from the knowl-edge of what I was about to experience: a strange land, sometimes a strange language, strange cus-toms. I would become the stranger, surrounded by strangeness. Exciting, certainly, but also fright-ening. All those small things I usually took for granted would become uncertainties—how to make a phone call, how to ease into a conversation, even how to turn on a faucet or an electric light. And in addi-tion to this loss of familiarity, there was also the chance of *being* lost, both geographically and psycho-logically.

Gradually, I realized that travel in itself is not happiness, but merely provides the opportunity for happiness in the most literal sense, the root of the word being "hap" as in luck, fortune, or serendipity. It could enrich, vitalize and extend the way I saw and thought; but it would do this not by making me happy but by challenging me. My work, of course, gave me the framework in which to discover this. But looking at other travelers, I would often see them suffering from the disparity between the advertised happiness of the travel brochures and the deflation of actual experience. Expecting happiness, it seemed to me, they had annihilated that vital element of "hap."

The idea that "hap" can be *made* to happen is a utopian one—an impossible ideal. Yet we still deceive ourselves, and allow ourselves to be deceived, that utopia is possible. Jonathan Swift's definition of happiness as "the perpetual possession of being well deceived" is as apropos now as it was when he wrote it.

Since it is as hard to be perpetually well deceived as it is to see with perpetual clarity, our guilt over not being happy makes the pursuit still more eager and desperate, and the quarry even more elusive. We can agree with Robert Burton when he wrote that "tis most absurd and ridiculous for any mortal man to look for a perpetual tenor of happiness in his life," and continue to be as absurd and ridiculous— and as mortal—as ever, puzzling at the goal we have set for ourselves like dogs frustrated by rubber bones.

The Once and Future Brave New World

The past always seems simpler, somehow, than the present. We can look back to two hundred years ago, and think that it seemed clear enough then what happiness was. It was established as part of the political, social, and personal system of rights in the United States. The New World was to be a happy society.

It was a revolutionary idea, a man-made promise to other men instead of a gift from the gods. But the Declaration of Independence promised a very different kind of happiness from the transcendent idea we now treasure.

When Thomas Jefferson wrote that famous phrase guaranteeing the right to the pursuit of happiness, he was being a hard-nosed politician: he meant primarily the right of citizens to pursue their own economic self-interest. Happiness was the freedom to run one's own life. Yet Jefferson's phrasemaking was to pave the way for what scholar Howard Mumford Jones was to call "a terrible misunderstanding—a confusion of public and private well-being . . . guaranteeing the American citizen the ghastly privilege of pursuing a phantom and embracing a delusion."

At first, the transition from independence to transcendence seemed unlikely. Politics had usurped the role of religion. Where once happiness was reserved for the next life, now it could be achieved in this one, if on a different order. Reason was to replace faith; utilitarianism would achieve what utopianism could not. From now on, happiness would be part of the order of nature and reason; its pursuit was legitimate. And unhappiness, by inference, was not legitimate. It became irrational, unnatural, and even un-American.

The trouble with the pursuit of happiness was that it imposed the burden of finding it. If the new society was working as intended, its individual members should be happy. The basic right to happiness thus gradually became the duty to be happy—or at least to present the illusion of it. Yet even when all the elements of political happiness were in place, people did not necessarily *feel* happy. Something seemed to be missing.

De Tocqueville sensed it as he traveled through America. "I saw the freest and most enlightened men placed in the happiest circumstances that the world affords," he wrote, yet "it seemed to me as if a cloud habitually hung upon their brow, and I thought them serious and almost sad, even in their pleasures." This hard-core seriousness with which Americans pursued their own welfare seemed to him the antithesis of happiness.

Pursued with such determination, happiness becomes something else all together: "no laughing matter," as Dublin's Archbishop Whately called it. It becomes easy to understand Mustapha Mond in Aldous Huxley's anti-utopian novel *Brave New World* when he sadly reflects on "what fun it would be if one didn't have to think about happiness." By making it into a duty, the element of spontaneity—one of its most essential aspects—had been destroyed.

But from the standpoint of the twentieth century, we prefer to ignore all this. Modern Americans no longer conceive of political happiness. Once there was a new society, a happy one, but now it seems to belong to another world—another society, more naive perhaps and simpler. Americans today look at their society and ask in disillusionment, "Was this the dream?" And they long for times past when everything was clearer, or at least seems so in retrospect.

There may be a basic conservatism in us all, not in the political sense but as a desire to conserve the past. The modern world changes too rapidly, we feel; even an intelligent newspaper reader may be hard put to keep up with who's who in which conflict at which time. This pace of change and the resulting confusion may in fact be no greater than at other tumultuous eras such as fourteenth- or seventeenth-century Europe; the major difference is our awareness of it. In the age of global communication, we have far more information than we know how to handle. Our own society seems unstable; so does the whole world. And above it all hangs the nuclear threat; the very idea of the possibility of global self-annihilation creates a general uncertainty vis-à-vis the future, not only as to what the future will bring, but even as to whether there will be a future at all.

If the global economy is uncertain, we know about it; if the American banking system is tottering, we know about it; if whole cities are changing, we know about it. Yet we feel helpless in the face of all this knowledge. Such problems seem too huge and unwieldy to tackle, even though they directly affect our lives.

Once, it seemed clear enough what American society was. But things that could be taken for granted just twenty years ago can no longer be. The American superiority in consumer goods has been lost to

West Germany and Japan, the very countries it defeated in World War II. The sphere of American influence in the world is being severely challenged in Central America, in the Middle East, and even in Europe. The Vietnam War radically altered the general perception of the United States as a defender of global freedom.

At home, Americans vie for European cars, French foods, and Japanese stereo equipment; they flock to Australian movies and British theater. As the sense grows that the country's natural resources are being depleted by the interests of big business, as unemployment and crime mount while the number of locks on city doors increases, as American public school education is revealed as less and less effective, the secure sense of rightness in being American is slowly being eroded. The values once taken for granted as the bedrock of American society are nearly all under question.

The same kind of "future shock" confronts us in our personal lives too. While 40 percent of American marriages end in divorce, challenging the very institution of marriage itself, "alternative life-styles" flourish. Unmarried couples see no reason to go through a marriage ceremony; gay men and women have claimed their right to homosexuality; more people are living alone in America than ever before. We can choose how we wish to lead our lives—or have them changed without choice—more rapidly and with greater ease. The very elements by which we define ourselves—who we live with, where we live, what we work at, how much we earn, who we admire or respect—are so vulnerable to change that it can feel as though we are in continual hesitation as to who we are.

This bewildering range of choice can be both exhilarating and terrifying; it places responsibility directly on the individual, and realizing this can itself be depressing. As a successful businesswoman who began her career only in her thirties put it: "There came a day when I realized that there was no deus ex machina in my life. Either I decided and acted, or nothing would happen. It was all me, not fate, and I was going to have to determine things for myself. I was depressed for weeks."

The social mores which would once have determined her life had disappeared; she was free of them, yet in limbo. If there was to be movement in her life, she would have to create it herself and take the risk of moving forward into an uncertain future.

Yet with all this uncertainty, Americans still believe in the pursuit of happiness. If anything, in fact, more than ever before. The social happiness envisioned by revolutionaries never quite worked out as they had hoped, and besides, it could never satisfy the stubborn human longing to transcend one's personal circumstances and to feel absolutely, wonderfully, deliriously happy. Happiness is still the American goal, but redefined with a vengeance.

The New Utopia

As though repelled by the unpredictability of the world and the unwieldiness of society, Americans have changed their focus. They have retreated into themselves.

The American dream has become intensely personal. The desire for the perfect self has replaced the desire for the perfect society. Utopia has been individualized; where once there would be a brave new world, now there will be a brave new self.

The new utopia has been fostered neither by the church nor by politics (though the weaknesses of both have contributed to its development), but by psychology and psychiatry. The new happiness will be found not through faith, nor through political action, but within one's own being. There at least, it seems, perfection might be possible. There at least the individual can aspire to some form of control.

It is basically a religious idea: if society cannot be redeemed, we can seek personal redemption instead. We can attempt to make ourselves "right"—"better" in some way than we were before, happier, closer to some perfect ideal of existence. The new religion is our selves.

There are countless churches in the service of this new religion, including over 140 different schools of psychotherapy (and those are only the ones in the mainstream). Each has its own idea of what will make us happy. In the past twenty years, we have spun through a virtual hall of mirrors of our potential selves. The perfect orgasm (the big "O"), self-fulfillment (dangerously confused with being full of self), growth and expansion of consciousness (might we eventually burst like overfilled balloons?), "whole-ness" (as though we were all multiple personalities), the perfect body (through diet or exercise, pursued with absolute devotion), the self-actualizing ego . . . All these and many many more, as the advertisements say.

Psychotherapy has become big business, creating its own demand through therapeutic hype. Promises of what we could be lead to vast dissatisfaction with what we are. We have become eager consumers of the new therapies, trying on the newest idea of self for size and then moving on to the next rack, to an even newer design for living.

Simple psychotherapy is no longer enough. Many people have now fallen victim to what has been called the salted-peanut effect, in which therapy creates the need for more therapy. One survey showed that 64 percent of people in therapy had been in therapy before with somebody else (and most of those in this survey were only in their twenties). Many engage in multiple forms of therapy simultaneously, apparently on the principle that more must be better. Between individual, group, and "growth" therapies, they wander from one "therapeutic experience" to another in a never ending quest for happiness.

Faith in the very idea of therapy does create short-term satisfaction no matter what the results. In the long term, more therapy becomes the obvious answer. Even psychoanalysis, the granddaddy of all the "talking cures," has gone beyond all reasonable limits. The original three- to five-year span has been unconscionably stretched by some analysts into ten or twelve years or even longer, making analysands into what are cynically known as lifers. And then there are such sad absurdities as the young woman who had been in analysis for three years; after that long, she wanted to know whether I thought her analyst was "the right one" for her. . . .

Meanwhile, a voguish, quasi-religious quasi-therapeutic movement has grown as western versions of eastern gurus come and go, offering perfect enlightenment and the illusion of age-old wisdom—a relief from the constantly advertised "newness" of popular psychology. Quick on the uptake, popular psychology has borrowed from them, promising joy, satisfaction, and a "secret" way to solve all our problems. Insights are turned into verbal Novocain, understanding into dogmatic faith. In eastern mysteries and western psychofads alike, we become first initiates and then converts.

Whether modishly eastern or scientifically western, the new gurus of the self are leading us along the road to perfection; in their ascent to the heights, the new converts look down with barely concealed superiority on those of us left to struggle with the problems of day-to-day life. "You have a problem, you know," is their classic riposte to those who dare question their perfect enlightenment. It is the ultimate putdown, since nobody wants to have problems anymore. That, they have already convinced us, is wrong.

Even psychologists succumb to the very illusions

they help create. Jerry Waters,* a professor of psychology on the West Coast, was once in the forefront of the avant-garde humanist movement which petered out in the tide of new-age therapies washing ashore in the seventies. Now he's in his fifties and adrift. "Being in psychology," he says, "and at my age, and with what I know, I should really have it all together. I *know* what having it all together could be. I *know* what being happy should be. But I just can't do it. It's very frustrating, frustrating and depressing." He has failed to live up to his own image—and that of his peers—of the fully realized individual.

"It's odd, you know," he continues. "I have a friend, also a psychologist, who has developed a set of 'life's laws.' His first law is: whatever you're selling is your tragic flaw. It's true. I have a very definite image of some people, somewhere, with impeccable mental health, happy and self-fulfilled, people who don't dwell on things but just go ahead and do them and are immensely successful and likable. And then there's me, feeling like that little guy in the Jules Feiffer cartoon, the one who's tried everything but only feels at home sitting right in the jaws of the dragon."

Unable to achieve the very ideal he helped propagate, Jerry's failure erodes his self-respect. Yet he still clings to the ideal, as most of us do.

Jerry was one of the many authors I read when I was still a student, eagerly sorting through a small multitude of definitions of mental health.

* All names of those talking about their own depression in this book are fictional, in order to protect the privacy of the speakers.

These were usually contained in inspiring last chapters of books on the breakdown of society and on human potential. Perhaps I thought that by simply amassing this wealth of insights in black on white, I could prove both to myself and to the world that perfection was possible. It did not occur to me then, being young and idealistic, that if anyone were actually to live up to these wonderful definitions of mental health, they would be literally inhuman—either nonhuman or superhuman. The idea that humanity was as much a collection of faults as of virtues would have been quite abhorrent to me. And in this I doubt that I was much more naive than most students of my generation. The early sixties were utopian years for both the young and the not-so-young. And none of us let go of the idea of utopia easily.

It was with some shock, then, that I returned to those definitions from my student days when I began research for this book. I found the source of what later became the "new age" in psychology and psychotherapy—the roots of psychobabble, which has reduced the study and practice of psychology to the consumption of psychology as though it were a panacea, the stomping ground for entrepreneurs such as Werner Erhard and L. Ron Hubbard. The key words in the old texts—humanity, authenticity, responsibility, self-actualization, potential—had all been voided of meaningful content by what came later. But the blame did not lie entirely with the Werner Erhards of this world.

To talk about authenticity and inauthenticity, as so many of these authors had twenty years ago, is one thing. But it is quite another when the underlying assumption is that "we," the reader and the writer, are the authentic ones, while "they," the masses somewhere out there in the big wide world, are inauthentic. And worse, somehow not quite human for that.

This was the new perfectibilism: to be fully authentic and fully human. And I was shocked by the very idea that human-ness could be measured. Yet there it was in the work of one of the greatest humanist psychologists of all, Abraham Maslow, one of the very men who most shaped my own thinking as a psychologist.

Maslow developed a test of self-actualization, on which humanity could be measured on a scale. "Full human-ness" was translated into quantitative terms, to be checked off on a list of attributes: the more you have, the more human you are—the fewer, presumably the less human. This checklist had the inescapable undertone of elitism—the superior conceit of the high scorers being able to say "I am more human than you. . . ."

In Maslow's defense, he was not unaware of the dangers of what he was doing. "You discover what a temptation it is to project your own values," he wrote, "and to make [the idea of mental health] into a self-description or perhaps a description of what you would like to be, or what you think people *should* be like. You'll have to fight against it all the time, and you'll discover that, while it is possible to be objective in such work, it is certainly difficult. And even then, you cannot really be sure."

No, you can never be sure of such definitions. And no, it is not possible to be objective. We are talking about the human mind, and we talk as human minds observing the human mind. This fact has been the bane of philosophy throughout its long existence (and the glory of literature). We are bound within our own subjectivity and by our own ideals.

If we can at least remember this, we might be able to avoid some of the major pitfalls of the pursuit of happiness. There are many responsible and insightful psychologists and psychiatrists who do remember it, but unfortunately they are outnumbered—at least in the public's attention—by those who presume to know what is right for us, promising us that we "need never be depressed again," in the words of one, and even offering us "the key to eternal happiness."

Feeling-Goodness

The evening's guest speaker, a smartly dressed man with an actor's smile, stepped up to the podium in the college auditorium. Carefully, he modulated his voice to the level marked "caring" and informed us that he would "share" with us a whole new approach that would completely change the way we lived our lives. He did not add that he had already "shared" this information, for a price, with thousands of others. Whatever his secret—and there always seems to be such a secret that can be communicated quickly and effectively—his assumption that he had found yet another gullible audience was profoundly insulting. I found it hard to resist interrupting the sharing with a cry of "Why don't you just *tell* us?"

But just to tell would not have that element of generosity and caring that he was trying to foster. Simply telling us would not indebt us to him as he urged us to "go with the flow." With the flow of what? "The flow of life," he said, eyes aglow with the light of self-satisfaction.

With the flow of violence? one might then ask. With the flow of poverty? With the flow of illness and disappointment, of shattered hopes and ideals, of loneliness and hopelessness, of separations and death and the other drastic changes that constitute the pattern of our lives?

Sometimes it seems that this is indeed what is expected of us. The new ideal is to be so caught up in our own psychic well-being that we ignore the fact that we live in a world of other people.

I wish I were exaggerating. But listen, for example, to Dr. David Burns in his book *Feeling Good,* one of the more popular books now on the market, as he tells us how we should feel when someone we love has died:

"You validly think 'I lost him (or her), and I will miss the companionship and love we shared.' The feelings such a thought creates are tender, realistic and desirable. Your emotions will enhance your humanity and add depth to the meaning of life. In this way you *gain* from your loss."

My first thought on reading this was "Thank God I am not loved by David Burns." What about mourn-

ing? What about tears and reproach of the world or
God for injustice? What about emptiness and hopelessness and the terrible awareness of the fragility of
life in the face of death? In other words, what about
the undesirable?

The new rush to "positivize" everything makes
even death and mourning into a matter of gain. If
your feelings when someone close to you dies are so
desirable, should you then wish them to die so that
you may have desirable feelings? The suggestion is
absurd, true, but it would seem to be the logical consequence of such an approach.

David Burns's idealized mourner is a narcissist
who is incapable of any deep feeling at all, or who
has to distort emotion into a "desirable" channel
before it can be felt. Such a person would be like
Voltaire's Dr. Pangloss in *Candide,* who imagined
that "all is for the best in this best of all possible
worlds." But Voltaire's irony has been lost. What
was once said in satire is now taken as gospel truth
and promoted as a new vision of mental health.

In Burns's world, the aim is to feel good. Feeling
bad is simply a problem, to be solved like any other
problem. It should be no surprise, then, that Burns
adopts corporate language to promote his system.
The aim of his book, he says, "is to help you devise
effective strategies to turn your problems around as
quickly as possible." He promises relief from all
symptoms of depression "in as short a time as twelve
weeks"—ignoring the fact that for most of us, depression passes within that time in any case, whatever
we do or do not do to alleviate the pain of it.

Personally, I find the idea of "turning my problems around" as though they were items on an order sheet quite abhorrent. Dr. Burns would no doubt say that I was merely being "occult and anti-intuitive" (an odd combination), since he claims that most traditional psychotherapy is so. But in fact if there is any occultism involved, it is Burns who is guilty of it. He promises us that by following his instructions closely we shall be "on the road to joy and emotional enlightenment"—and thereby sounds more like an eastern guru than a psychiatrist. Instead of science, or even understanding, Burns himself merely offers us more voguish and meaningless quasi-transcendentalism.

The purpose of it all, he says, is to promote his "mood-elevating techniques," based on the idea that we only feel bad because we're seeing things wrong, and if we can be made to see things "right," we'll feel good. Feeling good is not only feeling all right, it is seeing right and thinking right too. It is *being* right. And who then is to establish what is right to see and feel, and what is wrong? Burns assumes that he knows, but then so does Mustapha Mond, the director of Aldous Huxley's *Brave New World.* And we come dangerously close to seeing not only the world but ourselves too in terms of black and white, good and bad, allowing only certain thoughts and feelings as valid, and invalidating all others as wrong.

This brave new world assumes the terms of technology. We, like Dr. Burns, tend to think of our minds as capable of being programmed like a computer: feed in the right supply of positive signals, and out will come the perfect results. The increasingly technocratic society of the eighties demands results rather than reflection, and action rather than introspection. It emphasizes "breaking down" problems into their constituent elements, as though depression could be charted on a graph, diagrammed on a flowchart, and analyzed as easily as sales figures. Therapy becomes more like a business meeting than self-exploration, with therapists now trying to establish "life agendas" for their "clients."

If the goal is to be rid of depression, then depression is merely another problem to be broken down and solved. Just state your goal, and the experts will plan the way to achieve it. Most of our emotions—even our pleasures—have thus become "goal-oriented."

Where once we enjoyed our pleasures for their own sake, now they seem to be aimed at some ulterior purpose. We run in order to improve our hearts, we dance in order to lose weight, we study in order to pass exams, we read in order to keep up with dinner-party conversations. The sex-is-good-for-you movement taught us that sex existed in some area of life quite apart from relationship, liking, love, and respect. All pleasure is experienced at a remove—secondary gain, as it were.

When even pleasure becomes a matter of gain, then of course depression can only be wrong. It includes no elements that could be chalked up on a scorecard of achievement. It becomes a humiliating waste of time, and the very fact that we experience it erodes our self-respect.

Thus the novelist Joyce Carol Oates was driven to write an extraordinary essay in response to those who criticized her writing for focusing on sad topics.

Angrily, she asked, "What are we to make of the stubborn bitter truth that one's legitimacy is judged by whether one appears to be 'happy' or 'unhappy'? . . . 'Happiness' is predicated as a cultural norm, so that any deviation from it, however justified, arouses not only pity but reproach."

The search for perfection makes us intolerant of imperfection; the search for happiness makes us intolerant of unhappiness, even our own. Its very pursuit, worked at with such seriousness, has a pernicious effect on the way we see ourselves and others. We know it to be false—why else our endless fascination with the salacious details of the trials and tribulations of the rich and famous, those who we think have the best chance to be happy? Yet we stubbornly refuse to apply what we know to what we feel. That would mean a loss of faith in the ideal. Afraid to face that loss of faith, we concentrate on feeling good, and then feel guilty when we feel bad.

The Overlay of Depression

Unhappiness gives the lie to the socially accepted ideal of happiness. Its very admission seems to threaten the whole structure of the American ideal of "the good life"—the social consensus that happiness is possible and that we should try as hard as we can to achieve it. Unhappiness is hidden, even repressed, partly because others fear it as contagious and shun those who are unhappy, but also because it is socially unacceptable. "The depressed person shows up our whole social ceremonial by choosing to opt out of it," wrote social theorist Ernest Becker. "It doesn't interest him, its motivations are meaningless to him, its gratifications totally uninspiring. . . . It unnerves us that someone can be different to everything that we cherish."

To admit unhappiness is by now tantamount to an antisocial act.

At a party I went to, a well-groomed woman in her early forties clutched her whiskey glass close when she heard about my interest in depression, and without my asking her, said, "Oh, I've never been depressed, not really badly I mean. Well, except for once . . . That was when my brother committed suicide. Then I was depressed for months. But . . ." She paused, frowning, quickly finished her drink, and then looked up at me with a pleading expression: "But surely that was understandable, given the circumstances?"

That last sentence nearly took my breath away. The social intolerance of depression had forced her into an almost childlike plea for understanding, a plea which really said, "Tell me it was all right, tell me I wasn't crazy for mourning, tell me I wasn't sick for being depressed over the fact that my brother was so depressed that he killed himself. . . ."

There is no room anymore to respond to tragedy. If we do respond despite the social conventions against it, we only feel guilty, like the friend who called me one day "just to chat." She sounded strained and tired, though she chattered on about her work as a film editor and about a man she had met whom she was interested in. Finally, I asked what was really bothering her. Her mother had been rushed to hospital in a coma three days before, and the doctors had no idea what was wrong. "But you don't want to hear about that," she said. "It's so depressing. I've no right to impose all that on anyone else."

She had told nobody at work of this sudden crisis in her life. "What's the point?" she said. "They'd much rather not hear about it. So it's best to keep a happy face. I shouldn't be talking to you about it either, but I can't help it. . . ."

I thought of her a few months later, when I went to a conference on depression, organized for the general public as well as for professionals. I sat in on a workshop that included two young women who had been widowed within the last six months. Both were relatively young—one in her late thirties, the other in her midforties. And both had come for the same reason: they wanted to know whether they required professional help for their depression.

"All my friends keep telling me that I should get out and about, and meet a new man," said the one. "But I just can't bring myself to do it. So they suggested treatment." The second had received the same advice. "I just can't make myself merry and lighthearted at a party," she said, "and if you're not that way, then you feel you're being a deadweight, a drag. So I've stopped going out, and now my friends all are worried about me."

Even when someone *can* accept being depressed —as these mourning women did—friends and family feel threatened. "Go for treatment, *do* something about it," they say, as though if the feeling would only disappear, the event that gave rise to it would disappear as well.

Yet of course there is more to it than that. When someone else is depressed, we feel our own spirits sinking too. All the things we prefer not to think about—separation, death, loneliness, unhappiness—come crowding in, reminding us of when we felt that way, or how easy it would be for us to feel that way again. Devoted as we are to feeling good, our own capability for feeling bad seems like a transgression of faith.

Anyone who gets depressed thus inevitably feels guilty about it. A whole overlay of depression is created—not only the depression itself, but a complex structure of guilt, shame, and even terror.

We become depressed about *being* depressed.

The agony of depression often stems more from this overlay than from the original depression itself. If we were allowed to be depressed—if we could allow ourselves to be so—we might find it much easier to tolerate. But we cannot do that. A vicious circle of self-alienation is created, in which we are ashamed not only of being seen as depressed by others, but also of seeing ourselves that way. The social taboo against depression is internalized. The sense of "should-ness" is betrayed, for depression is never entirely personal; society is always watching.

The shame we feel presumes an outside observer—another's eyes in which we feel caught and guilty. When the overlay of depression sets in, we ourselves become that outside observer. We can do nothing without part of ourselves looking down and condemning it. We feel, and at the same time condemn ourselves for feeling. It is almost as though there were two selves: the self that experiences depression, and the self that judges that experience. Often, it seems easier to placate the latter than to tolerate the former. By repressing the experience of depression, we keep up appearances, even to ourselves.

Yet by denying depression, we deny ourselves; we deny our own experience, our own feeling. We assume that since we are depressed, we are invalid. And this assumption merely feeds into the depression itself, creating a further overlay of agony and self-blame. We *shouldn't* feel this way, we think, as though we really believed that we could become machines programmed only for the "right," socially acceptable emotions.

The Flight to Narcissism

Impatient with the complexity of living in the twentieth century, we wait for technology to simplify life. The urge to see ourselves in terms of "right" and "wrong," "functional" and "dysfunctional," is understandable: when the world is no longer simple, we can attempt to make ourselves simple instead.

As social analyst Theodore Roszak argued, "The tragic sense of life becomes a temporary discomfort; the dilemma becomes a problem. And like all problems that appear in the public realm, this too is presumed to have a solution . . . somewhere, somehow.

A technique, a medicine, a cure-all that will bring fast relief."

Yet if we could indeed manage our souls as we manage our business affairs, classify ourselves as we classify trees and plants, and determine our moods as we determine the flavors of ice cream, we would run the risk of ending up with only two or three flavors instead of the astonishing range we have right now. We would end up in a world where the only emotion is the tepid plasticity of no real emotion at all.

The ideal of never being depressed again, held out so temptingly (and so cruelly) by many popular books on depression, seems at first like a blessed relief. But on further reflection, it is more like a relief from life itself. It is another world, another order of being that is somehow lacking, chillingly unemotional.

Schizophrenics know this world. They have withdrawn into it, away from the whole realm of human interaction and relationship—even, in extreme cases, from the ability to feel physical as well as psychological pain. This is a state of severe emotional disturbance. Yet it is very close to the currently ideal state of no "negative" feelings. In this state, presumably, we would move from one relationship to another, one job to the next, one place to another, one age to another, with perfect ease, never taking time to sorrow for what has been left behind, or to feel the emptiness of loss of what has been. We would calmly accept change as though we were made of some jellylike substance that flows in whatever direction it is pushed.

Psychiatrist Robert Jay Lifton has called this ideal "the Protean man," after the mythic Greek character Proteus, the old man of the sea who could foretell the future. People would flock to him at noon, when he surfaced from the sea and sat on the rocks to bask in the sun. Anxiously, they would try to catch him and force him to tell the future. But no sooner would someone grasp him than he would transform himself into a different shape and wriggle free. Eternally changing shape, he told no futures.

This, says Lifton, is the new ideal—the constantly adaptable personality, never deeply committed to anything or to anyone, always perfectly changeable. It may be peculiarly well adapted to the exigencies of modern life, but this "psychological shape-shifting" makes for a vacancy in the heart—in the soul, even—characterized by a general sense of numbing, and lack of a larger meaning in life. Like the schizophrenic, the Protean man is guarded against the experience of pain. And also like the schizophrenic, there may be little sense of self left.

There are indeed some rare people who have never been depressed, but for the most part those who make this claim are either lying to themselves or to others—or suffering from a severe personality disorder. Never to be depressed is generally both abnormal and unhealthy.

Certainly there are people who seem to weather everything perfectly. They really seem to have achieved the impossible ideal. Yet . . . we begin to suspect something wrong. Could it be that everything seems *too* smooth? Too perfect? Could it be that

something is missing? Could what seems to be perfection in fact be narcissism?

With all the talk of narcissism and narcissistic
personalities over the past few years, the original
definition of narcissism has been lost. The "me" generation, the "culture of narcissism" explored by
Christopher Lasch, the "self-directed" focus of some
new-age therapies—none of these really refers to the
personality disorder psychiatrically known as narcissism. It is not "self-love," as commonly supposed
after the Greek myth of Narcissus falling in love
with his own image in the pool, but absolute and
complete self-reference, to the point where nothing
and nobody else matters.

The true narcissist often seems to have found that
ideal state of perfect equilibrium. His or her life may
conform to the social criteria for happiness, including even success, power, and status. Both that
person and others will be convinced of his or her perfection or even superiority. In the business world especially, such convictions count for a lot, and the real
narcissist may be extremely successful. This in itself
is enviable, but it comes at a price: a profound incapacity for genuine sadness or depression. Beneath
the often successful veneer, there is an echoing emptiness of all emotion—not only of depression but of
happiness too.

Narcissists relate to the world in a particularly
rigid way. Only they themselves—their bodies, needs,
thoughts, and everything related to them—are experienced as being fully real; everything else is experienced only intellectually, with no emotion. This lack
of depth and understanding means that the narcis-

sist has no sense of personal or social responsibility, and can exploit and manipulate others without guilt.

Yet this very narcissism is being advocated as the healthy ideal by some popular authors. Take psychiatrist Ari Kiev, whose book *The Courage to Live* sees depression in terms of "winning" and "losing." To be depressed, he argues, is to be a loser. And since nobody wants to be a loser in a world where at least the appearance of success is so highly valued, he promises complete "control over your own life and reactions"—a degree of control that the vast majority of his own profession would agree was the antithesis of any reasonable concept of a healthy personality.

Kiev's ideas are popular nevertheless, since who wants to appear weak, sick, or as a loser in a society based on appearances—and particularly, in the United States, on the appearance of self-confidence? We have neither time nor patience for crises of confidence such as those of depression. We are judged by how we appear. If we appear self-confident, then we *are* self-confident in the eyes of others (even to the extent that intelligent professional women could be convinced that "dressing for success" would make them successful). And if other people see us as confident in ourselves, they imagine that they are justified in placing their confidence in us. If we appear depressed, however, we fail: we lose not only confidence in ourselves, but also the concomitant confidence of others.

Politicians in particular are aware of this. Their careers depend on the appearance of self-confidence, and therefore the confidence of those who elect them.

Abraham Lincoln, for instance, would never have made it as a politician in today's world. He would have been stigmatized as surely and effectively as vice-presidential candidate Thomas Eagleton in 1972 when he revealed that he had been in treatment for depression.

Psychiatrist Ronald Fieve, whose book *Moodswing* plays on our fear of manic-depressive psychosis, would have taken strong measures with Lincoln if he had been able to. In his ideal world, we should all be in a state of equilibrium, with no jarring ups and downs to throw us off balance. If such things unaccountably insist on happening, the resulting emotion must be drastically uprooted. Here is what Fieve would have done about Lincoln's bout of acute depression in January 1841:

"His inability to attend the legislative sessions and the fear of his colleagues that he would attempt suicide would in modern time prompt most psychiatrists to arrange for inpatient hospitalization and treatment. I would insist on hospitalization, observation for suicidal intent, antidepressant drugs, and later administration of lithium as the treatment of choice for such a condition." And all this for what? For a bad depression that lasted a sum total of one week.

Lincoln was lucky that Fieve was not around in 1841. His psychiatric intervention would have deprived us of a brilliant and humane politician, and we would all—including Fieve—be the poorer for it. Yet despite Lincoln's example, and despite the tragic waste and rejection of men like Eagleton, we continue to insist that political candidates maintain, or at least appear to maintain, an impossible ideal of emotional equilibrium. We seem to expect that they be automatons who never experience any emotion in real depth.

The fact that we consider such men suitable for office is worrisome enough. Even more worrisome is the fact that we thereby ensure that we elect either dishonest men, who will not admit to such a thing as ever having been depressed, or scared men, who dare not do so, or men who repress their emotions to such an extent that any psychiatrist other than Fieve might diagnose a disturbing degree of emotional disorder.

Yet what we expect of our political leaders only reflects what we expect of ourselves. The politicians we elect mirror the values held dear by the majority of the electorate. We accept the illusion of their emotional infallibility not out of ignorance, but out of the desire to suspend our own disbelief in the ideal.

Reclaiming Depression

Two hundred years ago, claiming the right to be happy was considered a revolutionary move; in the late twentieth century, claiming the right to be unhappy may be just as revolutionary. We need to reclaim depression from the exclusive clutches of popular psychology, in which happiness and feeling good remain the only valid modes of human experience.

This is what Aldous Huxley's hero Savage does in

Brave New World. The inhabitants of that world float in a sea of shallow content created by Soma, "the happiness drug." But Savage, raised in the wilderness beyond the reach of this civilization and undrugged from birth, refuses it. "But I don't want comfort," he says. "I want God, I want poetry, I want real danger, I want freedom, I want goodness, I want sin."

To which Mustapha Mond, the director of this brave new world, sighs and acknowledges, "You're claiming the right to be unhappy."

Huxley saw that whatever the ideals we hold of happiness, it will always remain a matter of values. Happiness in itself is no guarantee of either health or desirability. A psychopath can be very happy indeed with a knife in his hand, as were Anthony Burgess's goons in *The Clockwork Orange.* A baby is all happiness as it stretches its hand toward the bright pretty colors of the fire in the open hearth. A heroin addict is happy when the drug hits the veins. Terrorists, oil tycoons, and even atom-bomber pilots may all be suffused with the pleasure that comes from self-esteem and belief in their actions—close, indeed, to the dangerous Nietzschean idea of happiness as "the most alive feeling of power."

Perfect equilibrium will always remain a tempting illusion. To be suffused with certainty, with satisfaction, and with the absolute conviction of one's own rightness seems quite enviable until we look at it closely. Then we see that nothing is quite so bland and inhuman as someone who is convinced that they have "found the answer." Think of the followers of a Rajneesh or a Charles Manson or an urban terrorist;

remember their glazed eyes, fixed smiles, and blithe blindness, as though all personal content had been sucked out of them in the same way that you can suck the contents out of an egg through a pinhole at the top. They seem dead psychologically, their minds given over completely to dogmatic belief. Yet there is no doubt that they are content, satisfied, and happy. Smugly so. All that is human and vulnerable in them is gone. They are capable of acting quite inhumanly, to family and friends as well as to strangers.

No matter how much we may desire personal pleasure we cannot allow the original idea of social happiness—the harmonious functioning of society —to be divorced from that of private and personal harmony. Pleasure in our selves cannot be the only value by which we lead our lives.

A responsible system of values will include depression. It is part of the process of deciding by what criteria we shall lead our lives and to what extent we shall allow ourselves the full range of human emotion.

The popular ideal of "getting rid of depression for ever" is only a Faustian bargain, surrendering feeling for self-alienation. If we want to lead lives that are meaningful, if we want to have a sense of continuity, to love and to belong, and to feel that life is worthwhile, we must also be willing to tolerate the depression that comes at times when reality betrays our desires.

Except at the severe extreme, there is no constructive or helpful point in seeing depression as illness, breakdown, or disorder. In fact, seeing it this way can be highly destructive. Rather, since it is a universal experience, we should see it as a normal reaction, and then ask what role it plays in our lives. If we consider it not as a problem but as a process, then I think we can appreciate that role, come to terms with our own feelings, and see them as a condition of being a sensitive, thinking human being—as integral a part of human experience as happiness.

3 *The Pressure to Repress*

Psychopathology is a contagious business. I clearly remember my first introduction to it, when I was studying psychology in England. The lecturer was one of England's top criminal psychopathologists, and since his classes were always at two in the afternoon, he came to the university straight from the pub, to which he had retired after a morning in court giving testimony. He was still dressed for court in a pin-striped three-piece suit, with a gold watch chain looped across his expansive stomach. His nose was invariably red from his lunchtime whiskey, which undoubtedly also helped loosen his tongue from the imposed caution of court procedures.

As expansive in his story telling as in his stomach, he would regale us with long accounts of cases he had dealt with, illustrating schizophrenia, manic-depressive psychosis, psychopathic personality disorder and so on with such vivid detail that we would all file out of the lecture hall convinced that we were suffering from whatever he had talked about that day. As the course progressed, we became schizophrenics, then manic-depressives, then psychopaths. Within the course of those two years, the entire class discovered that we suffered, sequentially, from every mental illness under the sun—and a few more that our fervid imaginations managed to produce independently.

It took time to realize that there are elements of craziness in us all, and that we can all resonate to some detail or other of a well-described psychiatric syndrome, generalizing from that detail to the whole syndrome.

In the same way, we can all identify to some extent with the case histories given in books on severe depression. After all, we get depressed too; we know what it feels like. But the danger is that these are the only accounts of depression available to the general public. And in the lack of any cohesive view of normal depression, we tend to imagine that we too must be severely depressed. Reading of cases and interiorizing the psychiatric categories, we make cases out of ourselves. Our fear of our own depression then intensifies and creates panic—a further element in the overlay of depression.

Seeing depression as pathological—that is, as illness—is a useful way of invalidating it. If it is illness, then it is not real, in that it has nothing to do with who we are or with how we live. It becomes a matter of fate rather than function.

The medical model of depression sees it as an entity unto itself, like any other illness. Depression becomes its own bacterium: an independent agent which takes over or "invades" the person, rather than an integral part of *being* a person. Like any disease, it is then something foreign, alien, and therefore threatening. And even though the whole notion of depression as illness was constructed on the basis of severe depression, psychiatry has generalized the idea to include every experience of depression, however mild or short-term by comparison.

A major part of this problem is that psychiatrists are first and foremost medical men. The requirements for qualifying in psychiatry—a medical degree followed by specialization in psychopathology—influence the way most psychiatrists think. Trained to take a medical attitude to the diseases of the body, they then transpose this same attitude to the ills of the mind. The mind must be diagnosed, treated, and cured in the same way as the body.

Those who have criticized this simplistic transfer of outlook are known as the "radicals" of their profession, since they question the fundamental assumptions of psychiatry. One of the best-known of these critics is Thomas Szasz, author of the now-famous *The Myth of Mental Illness,* who proposed that "the phenomena now called mental illness be removed from the category of illness and be regarded as the expressions of man's struggle with the problem of how he should live." The concept of mental illness, Szasz argued, "serves mainly to obscure the everyday fact that life for most people is a continuous struggle, not for biological survival but for 'a place in the sun,' 'peace of mind,' or some other meaning or value." Psychiatric categories such as mental illness and mental health, sanity and insanity, are merely labels, he argued. They contribute little to our understanding of the human condition, and serve merely to stigmatize those labeled as being on the wrong side of the psychiatric tracks.

Calling someone "a depressive," for instance, is a means of labeling that person. The person then becomes not someone who is depressed but the label itself: a whole role in life. One is a depressive in much the same way that one is a father, a doctor, or a Republican. But unlike those labels, the depressive one becomes intensely oppressive, trapping the person concerned in both their own eyes and those of the world. The world needs the label, not the depressed person.

The label wards off the depression of those doing the labeling. The truth is that depression *is* contagious, though not in the same way that physical illness can be. There is of course no bug or bacterium that carries it. Instead, the contagion arises because we are all capable of being depressed. Someone else's depression is thus liable to arouse our own and is threatening in that it mirrors our own. To prevent ourselves looking in this mirror, we label others as depressives and thereby determinedly hang on to a false status of nondepressed and thus "healthy."

For the depressed, this attitude merely reinforces their feeling that something is wrong and they are "not themselves." Something has evidently "come over them" from some outside source, a kind of invasion over which they have little control. Yet the lie of depression as illness is right there in the language. "I've got a cold," we say, or "I've got hepatitis." But we do not say—at any rate, not yet—"I've got a depression." Acknowledging it as a state of being, we say, "I am depressed."

We speak of depression as a state of being, yet try to think of it as a state of sickness.

Seduced by the idea of illness—since illness can presumably be cured, and then we would not have to be depressed—we choose not to acknowledge that there may *be* no illness in the first place.

Psychiatry has now taken over our lives to the extent that we rely on it to explain normal experience. But this is a contradiction in terms. Psychiatry deals with pathology, with the abnormal. The realm of normal human behavior and emotion has been claimed by psychology, but because depression has been identified as a psychiatric syndrome, psychologists have paid relatively little attention to the subject. Ignoring their own personal experience, they have for the most part assented to the psychiatric definition of all depression as malfunction. And in this, psychology has failed its purpose. It has left us without a working concept of normality for a universal state of mind, and forced us into seeing depression through exclusively psychiatric eyes, thus creating a problem where one does not necessarily exist.

"The Age of Depression"

Astonished by the sheer number of human beings delivered into their realm of expertise, some psychiatrists have even claimed the whole of human society as their province. This was particularly so in the late sixties and early seventies, when the "pathology of normalcy" posited by Erich Fromm enjoyed a long vogue in campus psychology courses. The fashionable claim was that society itself was sick and that therefore all its members had necessarily to be sick in order to survive in it. Suddenly, we were all neurotic.

The problem with this idea is that it was neither particularly original, nor particularly useful. Since nobody has yet produced an "un-sick" society except in the great utopian novels, we still have little notion of what a perfectly "healthy" society might be. Some theorists, Rousseaulike, have romanticized past ages and societies, conveniently forgetting the wars, epidemics, and repressive social systems that made life hard and short for most citizens. They argue that there is more depression nowadays because there is more social stress. But this simply does not hold up against the testimony: throughout all the written accounts of human history, from the time of King Solomon onward, we find depression.

Robert Burton, the seventeenth-century English churchman who spent years compiling the astonishing and often delightful tome *The Anatomy of Melancholy,* gave pages of quotes from the ancient Greeks and Romans bemoaning the pervasiveness of depression. Julius Caesar Claudinus called it "so common in this crazed age of ours that scarce one in a thousand is free of it." In Burton's own age, "we call him melancholy that is dull, sour, lumpish, ill-disposed, solitary, any way moved, or displeased. And from these melancholy dispositions no man living is free. . . . None so well-composed, but more or less, some time or other, he feels the smart of it." (Burton then gave what was presumably solace for his readers by listing foods to avoid since they aggravated melancholy. This list included beef, fowl, venison, milk products, fish, most fruit and vegetables, spices, grains, strong drinks, and beer. A naive reader might be forgiven for thinking that the only way to avoid melancholy was to starve.)

Whatever age they have lived in, people have seen their society as crazed and in a state of incipient breakdown. History lists vast numbers of false messiahs crying apocalypse and millennium, playing on exactly this fear and insecurity. Of course social and economic conditions can exacerbate depression; none of us live in complete isolation. But to say that a society is sick because its members are depressed is merely another way of invalidating depression, removing it one step further from the realm of meaning and experience. Depression is still made a matter of blame, whether one blames the individual or the society.

Nowadays, of course, there are statistics to prove the "sick society" thesis. In fact they prove little, since we have no statistical evidence from former times. The mania for numbers is a relatively recent phenomenon. Furthermore, those who refer to statistics to prove their point about the debilitating psychological climate of modern western societies are stepping on very thin ice. Any society's statistics will tell you more about that society's capacity and desire for statistical evaluation than about whatever the statistics are meant to represent. Suicide rates are astonishingly low in Catholic countries, for example, and depression is practically unknown in many Middle Eastern countries—not because there is none, but because there is no interest in assessing the rate of depression or, in the case of suicide, a definite interest in *not* assessing the rate. Even the statistically sophisticated United States produces contradictory figures, so that the current formula for severe depression is "seven to fifteen percent of the population"—a range that includes most of the different findings.

But in fact the current belief that this is "the age of depression" comes not from statistics nor from social theorists but from the drug companies, eager to promote their new antidepressant products. They have found a willing audience; ever since people have been depressed—which is ever since there have been people—they have sought means of denying the validity of their feelings by translating them into physical terms.

Hippocrates, the "granddaddy" of medicine, was one of the first to do just this, attributing depression to a surfeit of black bile in the body. (The word "melancholia" is itself Greek for black bile.) The black bile theory remained the basic paradigm of depression for centuries, part of the general system of the four humors which were believed to control all human emotions and temperament. It was the ancestor of modern chemical explanations of depression; both translate feeling into physical fact.

Black bile did have competition, however, mainly in the form of demons. Byzantine hermits in solitary desert cells struggled with these demons and were often conquered by them. They talked of the dreaded "noonday demon" who would tempt a monk with "hatred against the place, against life itself, and against the work of his hands, and make him think he has lost the love of his brethren and that there is none to comfort him." Under this demon's influence, they would stop praying and wander around disconsolately, spending their nights tossing and turning in torpid and restless exhaustion. It sounds like depression, but so far as they were concerned it was the demon, a clear exterior force that overcame them and in whose grip they were helpless.

The false adversary situation set up by the monks' refusal to look at their own depression made any hope of working through it very slight. Many went literally mad in the desert. But then of course it was the demons who drove them mad, not they who clung to an overly literal idea of good and evil, right and wrong.

The demons, in short, were very convenient. So was black bile. And so is modern biochemistry. All spare us the task of looking at our own lives too closely.

The irony is that the very term "depression" was coined so that we could take life experience into account. Until the early part of this century, melancholia was firmly established as a disease. Then in 1904,

Dr. Adolf Meyer argued that the term "melancholy" gave a stamp of certainty to a vague condition in which there was no positive evidence of disease. He proposed the term "depression" to differentiate between melancholy, or severe depression, and the more widespread kind that nearly everyone experienced. Life events were as relevant as organic disorder, he argued, and in most instances, the condition was related to life experience rather than to physical illness.

Eighty years later, the tables have turned. Now we think of melancholy as an almost delicious languor of mind and body. Influenced no doubt by the Romantics, we think of tall rather lean young poets languishing as they wait for love or inspiration, or preferably both. And depression, the word coined to denote normal experience as opposed to the sickness of melancholy, has become the new sickness.

The Health Neurosis

Everyone is afraid of mental illness. Physical illness seems simple by comparison. We know what to do about it, or at least we think we do. But mental illness remains baffling, beyond the realm of the acceptable. And yet, by giving all depression clinical status, we make ourselves mentally ill. Each time we experience it, we feel the sudden cold fear of being seen as "sick." "There must be something really wrong with me," we think at such times. "I need help."

"A little help from one's friends" at such times can

go a long way. But seduced by the psychiatric and big-business proclamation of the age of depression, we have lost faith in friends and in ourselves. If our problems are so severe, we think, we need expert help—the kind of help that often only reinforces the idea that we are sick.

Thomas Szasz angrily pointed out that "the demand for 'help' . . . is now met by a behavioral technology ready and willing to free man of his moral burdens by treating him as a sick patient." The whole of life can be translated into a psychiatric problem; there has been a psychiatric takeover of human existence so that all the problems of living, both the minor and the major difficulties of life, can be subjected to "solution." We have become consumers of psychiatry to the extent that, as Szasz wrote, "vast numbers of people—sometimes it seems nearly everyone—are deprived of a vocabulary of their own in which to frame their predicament without paying homage to a psychiatric perspective that diminishes man as a person."

We have become the victims of what ego psychologist Heinz Hartmann called "the health neurosis." We have reached the stage where our fear of sickness, fostered by the new technology of psychiatry, has made us neurotic about health.

People afflicted by the health neurosis cannot accept that they be anything less than perfectly healthy. Yet their idea of health is extraordinarily limited. It means "feeling good," "winning," "turning your problems around" in the minimum time, with minimum effort and pain. It means "complete control over your emotions"—a narcissistic idea of health that allows no room for suffering or for feeling depressed.

The new purveyors of mental health have even reduced the long and complex process of self-exploration through therapy to a package of instant weekend awareness, as though understanding came with a comic-book "zap." They have taken us into what Ernest Becker called "the myth of paradise through self-knowledge."

"The empirical facts of this world will not fade away because one has analyzed his Oedipal complex," wrote Becker, "or because one can make love with tenderness, as so many now believe." When psychology offers itself as a full explanation of human unhappiness, it becomes fraud, offering an impossible ideal as an achievable goal. The result is "therapeutic megalomania"—false expectations not only of cure but even of perfection through psychotherapy. This kind of mental health, said Becker, "is not typical but ideal-typical. It is something far beyond man, something to be achieved, to be striven for, something that leads man beyond himself." It is, in other words, a religious idea—a transcendent goal that can be reached only by saints or by those mad enough to believe themselves ultimately sane.

This obsession with an impossible healthiness has caused far more concern within the psychiatric profession than the popularizers would have us know. Psychiatrist Adrian van Kamm has even argued that the major goal of good psychotherapy should now be "liberation from the crippling influence of popularized psychological theories, from the tyrannies of anxious preoccupation with public image, and from the mistaken belief in the possibility of a 'scientistic' manipulation of human existence towards an almost magical readjustment to wholeness." And in his inaugural address as president of the American Psychological Association in 1979, Nicholas Cummings pointed out that "the mental health movement, in promising a freedom from anxiety that is not possible, may have had a significant role in the current belief that it is a *right* to feel good, thus contributing to the burgeoning consumption of alcohol and the almost universal prescription of the tranquillizer by physicians"—and now of the antidepressant too.

Much earlier in this century, Freud saw the health neurosis building and tried to counteract it. The business of psychoanalysis was not cure, he maintained, but the understanding and exploration of human experience. He had only the most general definition of health—"a healthy person is one who can love and who can work"—but it is a definition that still stands out as generously humane and nonjudgmental.

Many of his later critics and explicators have since accused Freud of fudging the issue of mental health. In fact he never did. "Healthiness is a purely practical concept," he told one of his students, "and has no real scientific meaning. It simply means that a person gets on well; it doesn't mean that the person is particularly worthy. There are 'healthy' people who are not worth anything, and on the other hand 'unhealthy' neurotic people who are very worthy individuals indeed."

A major part of the trouble has been the confusion

of healthiness, idealism, and normality. Freud too made this confusion. "A normal ego is like normality in general: an ideal fiction," he wrote. But the normal is not ideal; the normal is simply what exists.

What is normal is what is average. Normality is a statistical concept, and merely tells you what the average person—the one with 2.2 children, an income of $18,532.16, and a life expectancy of 75.3 years—believes, feels, or does. It is thus determined by what exists, and not by anyone's idea of what *should* exist. There *is* no absolute standard of normality. Nor, by definition, can there be one. Why then do we persist in maintaining that an ideal is normal, when normality is clearly very far from that ideal?

The ideas of desirability, health, and normality have been confused beyond any reasonable meaning. We want to be normal, or at least not to be too far outside the norm, since that is socially unpleasant, "undesirable." Normality is desirable, and since health is also desirable, normality is also health.

Yet the very fact of depression leaves no room in this equation for the ideal. Depression is certainly not desirable, yet since nearly everyone experiences it, it is certainly normal. Is it then healthy?

The very thought of healthy depression sounds like a throwback to the days when if the medicine tasted bad, it had to be good for you. The trouble lies in the fact that we have defined health in far too limited a manner. Feeling good, as we have seen, is no guarantee of health. Far more is involved.

Physical healthiness is the normal, active, independent functioning of the human body. This is what we mean by "a sound body." "A sound mind" can also be seen as healthy by this same criterion. Just as a sound body is capable of registering pain, so will a sound mind be capable of depression. The capacity to be depressed is part of being "of sound mind." There is no reason to call it neurotic or unhealthy.

As analyst Marianne Horney Eckardt has pointed out, we have spread the word "neurotic" over the whole rich and varied tapestry of existence: "Our implied norms are inadvertently judgmental. The flavor of the Protestant designation of sin reappears too often in the designation of the neurotic. Our norms tend to be conformist. They lack an imagination of the many ways in which life can have a sense of style, unity and integrity, even though it may be at odds with our notions of normality."

If nearly everything is dubbed neurotic, as it is by those who claim that we are all neurotic and that neurosis is the norm, then the remaining definition of health becomes inordinately narrow and bland. We need the salt and the savor of life that Jesus talked of in the Sermon on the Mount. This is not neurosis; it is life. The real neurosis lies in denying that and in insisting on an ideal of health so remote that we only make ourselves miserable trying to reach it. The unwelcome truth is that, as Heinz Hartmann saw when he analyzed the health neurosis, "the healthy person must have the capacity to suffer and to be depressed." Without that capacity, we become truly neurotic.

The Pressure to Repress

By labeling depression as neurotic, we push it out of the realm of valid experience, as though by so doing we could push it out of the realm of experience altogether. Of course experience wins out: we do become depressed. But then we are faced with the prospect of being sick and disturbed, even though the sickness and disturbance would often apply only if we were *not* depressed.

We lose tolerance for our own depression and evade it if we can.

John Matthews, for example, has been depressed quite often in the past couple of years and hates himself for it. In his early forties, he's well up the management ladder in a big corporation. His prospects seem good, and his income is already close to six figures, but the closer he gets to the top, the more he's aware of how fragile his position is. Like so many top executives, he is constantly maneuvering for survival. His divorce two years ago and his guilt about not being a good enough father to his two children add to the accumulation of stress. But the demands of his job leave no room for depression. "I should be strong enough to deal with it," he says, "should be strong enough not to let it happen in the first place. I mean, I should have more control over my own life. When I get depressed, I feel I have no control, even over my own feelings, and then I feel weak and degraded."

John's impatience with his own depression—his intolerance of it—reflects the current emphasis on control of emotions. He seems to expect that he be capable of a certain degree of inhumanity: *not* reacting as a fully sentient person, *not* reflecting on experience, *not* thinking in any meaningful or challenging way about the terms of his life. "Everybody else seems to manage okay," he says. So does he, at least to the casual acquaintance or observer. But that's not enough. What John really wants is "never to feel depressed at all. I'm tired of it. I want out of it."

He wants out of experience. And he could achieve that, certainly, but at a price. That price is repression.

Fear of depression and self-hate for being depressed drives much normal emotion underground. We quickly learn not to show depression if we can help it; from there it's a short leap to hiding our depression even from ourselves. Rather than feel it, we'll repress it. And in this we are encouraged by the society we live in.

When depression is stigmatized as illness and weakness, a double bind is created. If we admit to depression, we will be stigmatized by others; if we feel it but do not admit to it, we stigmatize ourselves, internalizing the social judgment. Many people then find that the only remaining choice is truly sick behavior: to experience no emotion at all when only deep emotion is appropriate. They will not allow themselves to be depressed.

We all play roles and wear masks to a certain extent, simply as a means of easing our way through life. Obviously how we feel is not everybody else's business. But it *is* ours, and when we are so afraid of coming to terms with our own business, the roles and masks we wear for others become all there is of ourselves. We wear them for ourselves too. Terrified of a bottomless pit of meaninglessness and depression if we let the masks slip, we struggle desperately to keep them in place.

Psychiatrists now talk of a whole syndrome known as "masked," "hidden," or even "smiling" depression. The mask they see may be psychosomatic disease or alcoholism or drug addiction—any state of being where psychological pain cannot be allowed into consciousness and therefore seeks expression in a physical way. Repression is as dangerous physically as it is psychologically. In the desperate quest to control feeling, the ultimate lack of control of slow self-destruction comes to the fore.

Masked depression works to a certain extent: the person concerned remains unaware of their depression. At its extremes, it is counterproductive, since alcoholism and drug addiction are socially unacceptable. But many people are walking a fine line of social acceptability with masked depression. A man with an ulcer, for example, is known as a hard worker. A man who drinks too much at home is simply under stress at the office and needs to unwind. There are now acceptable limits on the work use of cocaine and speed, and it's a rare office that has no Valium in a desk drawer.

"Sure I take something every now and again," says an account executive in a large advertising firm. "Everybody does; how else are you going to keep up? There's no time for moods and personal problems around here. You can't tell a client 'I'm sorry, I couldn't get the report done today because

I'm not feeling so hot.' " She shrugs, dismissing the subject as quickly as she can. "In any case, if you're really busy, you've got no time to be depressed." Or no time to feel it, at any rate. We can always make ourselves too busy to have time for ourselves.

Barbara Pirelli's life is far from that of Madison Avenue, yet she employs basically the same technique to avoid facing depression. When we talked, she was hustling around the tiny kitchen of her small apartment in a suburban clapboard house, making sandwiches for the Friday night poker game—a game when her husband, a construction foreman, gets sent out of the house "to go drink with the boys. Friday night is for the girls."

The boys and girls are all in their late fifties by now, and like most of her friends, whom she's known throughout her life, Barbara has never held a paying job. But she spends hectic days outside her home: volunteer work with the scouts, with local hospitals, with charity organizations; hiking, roller-skating, and trailer clubs. "I keep busy," she says, nodding firmly. "When I hit the pillow at the end of the day, I go out like a light because I've been so busy. Maybe I'm doing it on purpose, being so busy, but I never slow down to find out."

I've been in her house a couple of hours, and she still has not sat down. When I point this out to her, she makes coffee and then sits briefly at the table, crocheting in her hands. What would happen if she slowed down?

She shrugs. "I'd start thinking, wouldn't I? Things you're not supposed to think about. Worrying, you know . . . Thinking about different things." But she shies away from those "different things." "Something bothers me, I get down on my hands and knees and wash down the steps or whatever. I've got no time for bad thoughts."

Most of the time it works. But then came the time when she broke her leg and couldn't move around for a while. "I wasn't doing anything, just sitting around at home, and I started feeling real sorry for myself, thinking about what's happening to the kids, if they're happy out there in the world and so on. Thinking about Len and worrying about him hurting himself at work. Thinking about myself and . . ." But she won't talk about it, even now, years later.

It was her daughter who told me how depressed her mother had been at that time, how things had piled up inside her so that they came out with explosive force when she was suddenly immobilized, terrifying both Barbara and her family as she screamed at them, cried, smashed dishes, and then withdrew into silence. When the leg finally healed, she threw herself back into busy work, more frenzied than ever. "You've got to keep moving," she repeats as she goes back to the sandwiches and begins to cut all the crusts off them. "Else all kinds of things can happen."

The fear of depression can mean that, like Barbara, we spend much of our lives in the frantic attempt to evade it. It's nothing new; Shakespeare wrote that "Sorrow concealed, like an oven stopped, Doth burn the heart to cinders where it is." But such evasion is dangerous. Though repression may make our lives smoother and easier in the short run, in the long run it demands too high a price. It seems both saner and healthier to be depressed. Yet for men in particular, this conclusion is practically unacceptable.

Feminizing Depression

"There is something about a man in tears," says psychologist Herb Goldberg, "that offends, causes others to turn away and to want to 'do something' to stop it as soon as possible. Tears from a woman bring out a protective feeling. From a male, tears create discomfort at best and occasionally even mild disgust at his inability to 'control himself.' Manliness is still equated with poise and composure in the face of tragedy."

Depression, with or without tears, is seen as a very feminine state of being.

The recent spate of books on women and depression has merely reinforced this attitude, since all take as their starting point the fact that women are treated for depression two to three times as much as men. Criticizing these findings, some feminists have claimed that psychiatrists slap the label of depression on women because they see them as weak. Thus these feminists also assume that to be depressed is to be weak.

But the assumption that women *are* more depressed than men never rang quite right for me. I kept wondering what was happening with the men. Were men really "healthier" than women, as these findings seemed to indicate? Or were women simply more open about depression?

As I began research on this book, I was quickly set straight on the issue—by men themselves. Many seemed to be almost insulted that anyone should think they did not get depressed too. And they were even more relieved than the women I spoke to at being able to talk about their depression to someone who evidently did not consider it a sign of illness or of lack of masculinity. In fact, most of them rushed in to claim in-depth experience on the subject, using remarkably similar phrasing to indicate how much they knew:

"Oh God, you could write a whole book just on me," was a common response (others, more modest, claimed just a chapter). "That's one subject I can tell you everything you need to know about," was another. But the most common—so much so that after a while I could hardly repress a smile when someone said it—was "Oh yes, you're talking to a professional."

Such claims to professionalism and exhaustive knowledge were generally exclusively male responses. Women rarely responded this way; they tended instead to smile a little sadly, nod, and anxiously ask, "Would you like to interview me?"

Behind the men's claims, it seemed to me that what they were really saying was "We too are human; we also get depressed. You should only know how much." And indeed I can sympathize with this, because when the claim is made, as it was by Maggie Scarf in her book *Unfinished Business*, that women get more depressed than men because they have a special need to be nurtured, one cannot help wondering what such ideas imply about men. Do they not need to be nurtured too? Are they in such control of their emotions as the stereotype would have them be?

The current rush to research female depression allows no answers to such questions. Not only does it ignore the universality of experience, but it further feminizes it, making it still more difficult for men to admit to. In fact, the feminization of depression is an insult both to women and to men—to women because it makes them seem as though they were somehow "sicker" and weaker emotionally than men, and to men because it dehumanizes them, ignoring their emotions in favor of a questionable statistic.

The truth is that the statistics on women and depression do not show facts about depression so much as social and cultural trends that hide the full story by forcing men into repression for fear of being seen as feminine.

Perhaps the most dramatic and thought-provoking research on the issue of mental health and socio-sexual roles was that done by Inge Broverman of Massachusetts's Worcester State Hospital and her colleagues. Their stated aim was to determine what people thought constituted mental health. One group of those surveyed was asked to select desirable personality traits for "a mature, healthy, socially competent adult person." A second group was asked to do the same thing, except that the word "male" was substituted for "person." And a third group was asked to select criteria for "a mature, socially competent adult female." The results were astonishingly clear-cut.

First, it was clear that people's ideas of a mentally healthy man were very different indeed from their ideas of a mentally healthy woman. But more, the image of the mentally healthy man was very close to that of the mentally healthy *adult.* The criteria for male mental health were practically the same as those for adult mental health—while the criteria for female mental health were radically different from either. A healthy male was a healthy adult, and a healthy female . . . something else.

The inescapable conclusion is sadly familiar: not only do we have different cultural, social, and individual criteria for mental health in men and in women, but we see the male standard as healthier than the female one.

One further factor was perhaps even more disturbing: the people asked to define mental health in this survey were not members of the public at large; they were clinically trained psychologists, psychiatrists, and social workers, most of them with Ph.D. or M.D. degrees. They were the very clinicians who determine whether someone is healthy or sick, depressed or not depressed. If their standards of mental health were so hopelessly distorted by biases, preconceptions, and stereotypes about male and female behavior, then any figures based on their classifications and evaluations would suffer the same distortion.

Since clinicians too are human, it is not entirely surprising that they should share the prejudices of the rest of the population. They do indeed diagnose depression more easily in women that in men, because they see both depression and being female as states of weakness. They reflect the social consensus that it is more acceptable for a woman to be depressed. And thus women feel freer than men both to report depression to researchers and to seek treatment for it.

In this, women are absolutely right. They are judged by different, far less severe standards than are depressed men.

Through the seventies, psychologist Constance Hammen of the University of California at Los Angeles worked with a number of colleagues studying depression among college students, and found that "the negative consequences of expressing depressive responses may be strong and unambiguous for college males."

Depressed college men are seen by their peers as much more disturbed than depressed women, for instance. They are rejected more as friends, partners, and co-workers. They are seen more negatively than depressed women. But they are also seen as more feminine than other men. Men can tolerate other men's depression and women other women's, the researchers found, but both sexes are far less tolerant of depression in the opposite sex. And women are far more severe judges of depressed men than vice versa, so that if a man is depressed, he loses his "sex appeal."

Hammen and her team found that men and women got depressed to an equal degree, but were very different in the way they expressed it. Women are more likely to express it overtly, crying and talking to others, and blaming themselves for being depressed. Men try to repress it; many withdraw from others, becoming tight-lipped and uncommunicative as though silence could disperse pain.

Sexual stereotyping of depression thus victimizes both men and women. It reinforces the stereotype of women as weak, unable to control themselves, and irrational. And it constricts men by denying them a normal emotional outlet. Since it threatens their sexual identity, men are more afraid of depression than women; forced to live up to the masculine imperative, many block their own experience. Others, facing the choice between being inhuman and being unmanly, simply feel trapped.

The Male Dilemma

"It's hard when you're depressed, because it means you've failed. You're less of a man somehow. You know this isn't rational, but that's how it is."

Jack McBride is a top editor on a major weekly publication, and seems to have an enviable enough life: his second marriage is working out fine, his job is as secure as any job can be these days, he lives in a desirable neighborhood, and is on good terms with his first wife and their children. But still he gets depressed from time to time, and when he does, he feels that despite everything he has failed.

He singles out four times that the depression was really bad, the times when he "seriously considered suicide": when he was passed over for a promotion, when he flubbed an important assignment, when his first marriage broke up, and when he realized that he would never get the post he most coveted at the magazine—"all times when I realized that I wasn't going to be able to do something I'd wanted to do, and that there was nothing I could do about it; all times I was impotent."

Depression is often experienced by men as an attack on their potency, both literally and metaphorically. Since it is deemed unmanly, other attitudes about being male come into play, aggravating the depression. This is undoubtedly what happened to Ernest Hemingway, who presented himself as the quintessence of manhood yet still had to deal with what he called his "black-assed days." As the self-styled American hero, Hemingway forced himself into a corner where the conflict between being stereotypically male and being depressed became intolerable, and suicide seemed the only way out—with a shotgun, of course.

Fortunately, most men are less concerned about their maleness than Hemingway, or less anxious about it. Except at times of depression.

"I feel trapped when I'm depressed," says Jack McBride. "I should be able to *do* something, and I can't. It makes me feel really unmanned—I should be out there doing all kinds of things, and there's nothing I *can* do. And then on top of that I have to make like everything's just fine, else I'll lose face. I can't let anyone *see* that I'm depressed, because that'll only make things worse. They'll come down on me all the harder then, like wild animals turning on a sick member of the pack."

In the world of the masculine imperative, loss of

control is taboo and therefore punishable. This taboo against expressing depression forces many men into schizoid behavior: feeling one way, they are forced to act another. Just as schizophrenics withdraw into themselves, away from what seems to be an unmanageable world, so do many men withdraw when depressed, unable to live up to their own image of manliness yet equally unable for the moment to do anything about it. They are caught in the double bind between image and reality.

Most women would then ask why men don't do what women often do—seek out a friend to talk about it. But very few men can. The masculine imperative places a high value on going it alone; seeking help, even from friends, is a sign of weakness. What seems like a natural outlet for women simply does not exist for most men. They will talk with each other about business, baseball, politics—anything except what really ails them.

Since I am accustomed to the ease with which women talk to each other about their feelings, it still amazes me how very little men confide in each other. Even turning for professional help in the form of therapy is seen as a "feminine" activity, since it means giving up the illusion that everything's under control. As Herb Goldberg put it, "if he asks for help, he impugns his masculinity; if he goes it alone, he crumbles under the weight."

The result is frightening. Repression can kill, both slowly and suddenly. For instance, while women receive hospital treatment for depression twice as much as men, men receive hospital treatment for alcoholism—a classic form of masked depression—four and a half times as much as women. And while women attempt suicide four times as often as men (attempted suicide now being seen as a form of plea for help), men actually commit suicide three times more than women. Instead of being expressed as conscious feeling, depression either leaches to the surface in the form of slow self-destructiveness, or explodes suddenly and violently as in suicide.

We wrong ourselves by denying and repressing depression. Burdened by stereotypes and impossible ideals, we deny the validity of our own feelings; in fact, we deny what we feel.

4 Being Depressed

"From these melancholy dispositions, no man living is free, no Stoick, none so wise, none so happy,
none so patient, so generous, so divine."

ROBERT BURTON, 1628

The basic feelings of depression are familiar to us all:
the feeling that there is no point in life; the feeling of
exhaustion, of having no energy; the feeling that life
is just one long struggle and that the rare moments
of happiness are just not enough.

We feel heavily apathetic at such times. The most
menial tasks become hard to do. Even shaving or
brushing teeth becomes a chore. Our bodies feel
heavy and sluggish, as though the life energy had
been drained from them.

"I'm totally exhausted when I'm depressed," says
a midwestern college teacher. "Everyone else seems
to have so much energy, and I have none. All I want
to do is sleep. I hear it in my voice, and I see it in the
way I stand or the way I walk—you know, when you
walk past a store window and think 'Who is that

depressed-looking person?' and then realize that it's you. It feels like I'm dragging around a huge burden all the time, and I can't get out from under it."

A West Coast electrician feels "stuck when I'm depressed. It's an oppressive kind of feeling. I feel very trapped. Not because I don't know what to do, but because I can't seem to come up with the engery to move, to get out of it, to change what I know needs to be changed. And the struggle against that feeling is exhausting in itself."

His feeling of entrapment is echoed by a businessman who feels "like I'm in a black box, a small black box, with just enough room to flail around in but not enough room for anything else." The flailing around is because "as I've experienced depression, I have a sense of pressure to do something without feeling the *ability* to do anything. I feel 'do-less,' with very low energy, and then also guilty because I'm not doing anything."

Many people feel almost literally deflated at such times: "like all the air's gone out of me," "like I'm heavy all over," "like I'm spread out on the ground and can't get up again." We feel irrevocably earthbound. Everything weighs down on us, making the body feel as heavy as the spirit. It is as if some kind of psychic puncture had deflated the balloon of wellbeing and left the sense of self collapsed in a heap by the side of the road. "It pulls down inside me and I feel it physically, like the wind's gone out of me," as one woman put it. "I feel sort of amorphous, shapeless."

At such times, we feel robbed of desire. Food loses its taste, sex its appeal. The basic hungers of life fade into nondesire. If we satisfy them at all, we do so mechanically.

One of the most vital feelings of aliveness, for instance, is not so much the satisfaction of hunger, but the *being* hungry, especially if one has the certainty that this hunger will soon be satisfied. That moment, for example, when you come home starving after a long hike in the woods, and smell food being prepared. As soon as it is ready, you wolf it down, and it seems the best food you ever tasted. And then there is the feeling of satiation, but also a strange moment of longing for the hunger now gone, for the sheer joy of being alive and hungry and about to eat. It often happens this way—that in a state of anticipated satisfaction, we feel better and more alive than in the satisfaction itself, more awake and attuned to the details of the world around us.

In depression, however, this cycle of need—of anticipated satisfaction and of pleasurable fulfillment—is flattened out. As though weighed down by a huge press, all human desires become a monotonous continuum. Cut off from satisfaction, we feel cut off from need itself. It is as though everything tasted the same, with that one taste barely perceptible.

Soon, the depression seems to take over all our thoughts. We seem to see everything "through a glass darkly." We focus on bad news—on murders and disasters, wars and poverty, suffering and misery—and become convinced that this is all the world consists of.

At this stage, some people feel deeply threatened, as though they were drowning in depression. A nurse talks of "being a very small person and seeing this huge wave, like a tidal wave, that's going to come and drown me, so that I'll be swept away by it and destroyed." Others speak of being sucked down into depression as into a whirlpool, of struggling to stay afloat, of sinking or floundering or fighting for air. All express the fear of the deep, and emphasize the helplessness of feeling out of their element, struggling against something that threatens to overwhelm them.

However short or long a time the depression lasts —whether hours, days, or even weeks—we soon become convinced that we shall never emerge from it. We may even terrify ourselves by thinking of the possibility of suicide. And yet, sooner or later, it passes, and we return to what we think of as normal life.

For some people, this has become so familiar that it is a strange kind of friend, a dark and familiar presence always waiting in the wings. For others it is far rarer—discrete times that stand out as unusual in the memory. As William James observed, all it need take is "a little cooling down of animal excitability and instinct, a little irritable weakness and descent of the pain threshold," and that will "bring the worm at the core of all our usual springs of delight into full view, and turn us into melancholy metaphysicians."

Even the experts are no exceptions. Freud's biographer Ernest Jones wrote that Freud was often depressed, and that at such times he "could neither write nor concentrate his thoughts (except during his professional work). He would spend leisure hours of extreme boredom, turning from one thing to another, cutting open books, looking at maps of ancient Pompeii, playing patience or chess, but being unable to continue at anything for long—a state of restless paralysis. Sometimes there were spells where consciousness would be greatly narrowed: states, difficult to describe, with a veil that produced almost a twilight condition of the mind."

Times hangs heavy. There is simply too much of it. The future stretches out with infuriating length, holding no promise or new possibility. Where the happy person is often blissfully unaware of time, sometimes even childlike in amazement that something good can be over so soon, in depression we have an all too adult awareness of mortality and finiteness. Like our own selves, time seems empty.

The Empty Self

"The lack of possibility is like being struck dumb," said existentialist philosopher Søren Kierkegaard, "for without possibility a man cannot, as it were, draw breath." When the future offers no new possibilities, a paralysis of conception sets in.

Where happiness involves such complete confidence in the future that it hardly even needs thinking about, depression involves a complete lack of confidence in it. There can only be more of the same, we think, whether that be the agonizing helplessness of despair or the grinding monotony described by the Greek "poet of Alexandria," Cavafy:

A month passes and ushers in another month.
One can easily guess the coming events;
they are those tedious ones of yesterday.
And the morrow ends by not resembling a morrow.

But because we lack confidence in the future, we do not necessarily lack confidence in our ability to survive. Physical survival is less the problem in normal depression than the worth or value of that survival. The question is not whether to be, but *how* to be. And this question inevitably involves the future. It involves a projection of current circumstances and intention into the future. It involves purpose.

In recent years, any consideration of people as creatures directed toward the future has been devalued to some extent by the prevailing influence of the "here and now" philosophy, which mimics the time sense of happiness by bringing everything into the present. But meaning and self-esteem are based not only on what we do right now, but also on what we have done in the past and can imagine doing in the future.

When we are depressed, this projection into the future is blocked. In a sense, depression is a temporary dead end in life. The sense that life holds nothing more and that there is no point to existence constitutes a sense of completion.

"When I'm depressed I just don't want to get up in the morning," says a young sales executive. "I go into the bathroom, look at myself in the mirror and ask myself what's the point in shaving, what's the point in anything at all? Everything seems routine, meaningless." There is no dynamic, no futurity, no sense of progress; and this is the metaphor of death. While in happiness one feels more alive than ever, in depression the feeling is one of being "dead to the world," "at a dead end," "deadened," or "numbed." There seems to be nothing to wish for, and as Rollo May has pointed out, "to cease wishing is to be dead, or at least to inhabit a world of the dead."

The paradox is that we feel this deadening and numbing acutely. There is a painful intensity which is quite the opposite of the total absence of feeling in death. The questions "Why?" and "What for?" are superbly human—exclusively human, in fact. Without an answer to them, existence in the present seems pointless and empty. Not only is the world empty, but so are we.

It is one of the most basic feelings of depression: blank, nothing there, empty of all meaning. It can feel as though there were suddenly a huge hole in the identity—a black hole like those in space, which seems to grow until it engulfs everything within its reach, converting everything solid into nothingness, our whole lives into emptiness. As a woman who had just suffered a series of tragic deaths in her family finally put it, "I can't believe how strongly I feel nothing."

It is of course a contradiction in terms. To be overwhelmed by emptiness is surely to be overwhelmed by nothing at all. The very idea would make no sense to someone who has never been depressed.

R. D. Laing described it this way: "Nothing, as experience, arises as the absence of someone or something. No friends, no relationships, no pleasure, no meaning in life, no ideas, no mirth, no money. Emptiness. Take anything and imagine its absence." But it is still more than this. It involves not only the absence of that person, thing, or quality; it involves the absence of it in *you*—the absence of that part of yourself that was connected to what has been lost. Not only are there no friends, no meaning, or no pleasure, but that part of you which finds friends, meaning, or pleasure seems itself to have been lost. It seems as though you will never again be capable of such things—as though the emptiness were a permanent negative entity instead of merely a phase. At such times, you enter a vacuum in which nothing except the vacuum itself can be taken for granted.

This vacuum is all the more difficult to bear because of the popular emphasis on "fulfillment"—literally, being filled full. If fulfillment is good, then emptiness can only be bad. Worse, it becomes confused with impoverishment. The terms of financial currency are translated into emotional currency.

For most people, economic security is part of the bedrock of happiness. But for too many, it becomes the structure of happiness too, as though financial riches could secure emotional riches. (A point on which P. G. Wodehouse had his usual quirky say in *Quick Service*. The hero responds to the advice of his beloved that money doesn't bring happiness with "True, but on the other hand, happiness doesn't bring money; you've got to think of that too.")

Economic security becomes so effective a symbol of psychological security that the symbolism itself is soon forgotten and the one becomes the other. Impressed by the power of money to earn at least the exterior trappings of happiness and security, we use economic terms to talk about our emotions.

"Sure, when I feel down and insecure, I feel really impoverished, like there's less of me," says Bea Castelli, an administrative assistant who has spent a lot of time "working on herself" in various therapies. "I think 'poor me, poor Bea,' like I'm really to be pitied, and I start identifying with all the poor people I see around me, with the bag ladies especially. I see them and I think 'That could be me, that's how I'm going to be if I go on like this.' But then when I'm feeling really good, I don't even see the bag ladies. I really do feel full of myself, the whole of life seems rich, and it's like I'm so full that I'm brimming over with all sorts of good feelings, like there's plenty of me to spare, if you know what I mean."

One time when there is absolutely nothing to spare is when we are physically exhausted, whether because of overwork, ill health, or enforced immobility. The physical depletion of energy is then often mirrored in a felt depletion of psychological resources. Just as depression makes us feel physically exhausted, so can physical exhaustion create depression. The question of energy is more than symbolism or metaphor; it is part of the subtle and complex interplay of mind and body.

Take, for instance, the word "tired," which we often use as a synonym for "depressed." We can be tired of work, tired of parties, tired of a person, tired even of living. Nothing seems to have any point; everything drains energy. We are bored, and the boredom itself is exhausting.

Boredom may be a far larger element in depression than most of us care to admit. It parallels depression in many respects: the tiredness, the sense of time moving slowly, the inability to move, the lack of interest and sense of emptiness. But it has a sharp jagged edge to it that depression usually does not. It doesn't have that sense of deflation and of acknowledged helplessness so common in depression. But it may be all that a person will allow themselves to feel of depression. To be bored does not seem as terrible as to be depressed. As psychiatrist Willard Gaylin points out, boredom may be used "as a defense against our own emptiness. . . . Perhaps the trivial use of so plebian a word as 'tired' is our way of avoiding the implications of the feeling."

In boredom, we are passive but agitated, restless, and irritated. In depression, the passivity is more introspective; instead of covering over the feeling of emptiness with restlessness as in boredom, we allow ourselves to feel it. For many, boredom might then be preferable, because what we feel is what T. S. Eliot called "a loss of personality." As the mysterious guest says to Edward in Eliot's play *The Cocktail Party,* after Edward's wife has suddenly left him:

Most of the time we take ourselves for granted,
As we have to, and live on a little knowledge
About ourselves as we were. Who are you now?
You don't know any more than I do,
But rather less. You are nothing but a set
Of obsolete responses.

It is a harsh judgment but painfully correct. When you are depressed, you feel bereft not only of what was dear, but also of your own accustomed self. You are left clutching at threads that lead nowhere. Nothing can be taken for granted any longer.

We all feel this way at one time or another, and still we wonder, "Is it normal?"

The Definition Dilemma

Much as we hanker for an easy handle by which to grasp depression and understand it, it evades any simple definition. There is no way of saying "Depression is . . ." as though you could just fill in the rest of the sentence in twelve words or less and win the prize advertised on the back of the cereal box.

Depression is a complex range of human experience, and simplistic statements about it are, simply, misleading. Despite the vast range of research on the subject, even psychiatrists cannot agree as to what it is. It has been called a mood, an affect, an illness, a "basic state," a character style, a symptom, a syndrome. . . . In spite of its ubiquity, or perhaps because of it, each writer defines it differently.

Sometimes the emphasis is on the pessimism, sometimes on the fatigue. Some experts emphasize the feeling of meaninglessness, others the sense of helplessness or hopelessness. And though they rarely say so, most psychiatrists tend to define depression according to their own experience of it. As analyst Myer Mendelson tactfully put it in introducing an anthology of papers on the subject: "It is now clear that the term 'depression' covers a far wider range than was previously thought, and for different writers 'depression' has not only different components but different purposes."

Some have tried to avoid this problem by couching their definitions in such generalized terms and such bad English as to defy comprehension. Try this for example: "The phenomena of depression must be viewed as a multilevel spatiotemporal pattern of events occurring in genetic, biochemical and interpersonal systems." Trying to please everyone, this particular writer ended up saying nothing.

To exacerbate the problem, nearly all writers are still concerned almost exclusively with severe depression: the depression of psychosis, the hospital ward, and antidepressant drugs. In fact, the idea of normal depression was scarcely mentioned in professional papers until the mid-thirties. Even then it was dubbed "mild" or "neurotic"—terms which kept it securely within the psychiatric realm, and thus defined what is normal as abnormal. Further confusion has been caused by the fact that mild or normal depression can be experienced very acutely—far more acutely, sometimes, than severe depression, which may often be marked by a deadening inability to feel anything at all.

More recently, a new term has entered the language: clinical depression. But though it has a coldly definitive ring to it, clinical depression really means only one thing: depression that has come to the attention of a clinician, whether it be a psychiatrist or a psychotherapist, an analyst or a regular physician. It has no meaning beyond the fact that someone has sought professional help, and that in itself is no indication of severity.

Just as people have varying tolerances for physical pain, depending on circumstances and personality, so they have varying tolerances for psychological pain. There are also cogent sociological reasons why those with higher education, for example, seek clinical help more quickly, or why women seek it more than men. The figures for clinical depression thus tell us relatively little about the real incidence of depression.

The result of all this is a strange anomaly. Each one of us knows what we mean when we use the word "depression," since each of us knows it from first-hand experience. Yet attempts to define it concentrate almost exclusively on a small sector of the population, those who are clearly severely depressed. Even for this small sector, there is no agreement among experts as to what it is. And the various definitions available seem to be influenced as much by the personality and psychiatric politics of the definer as by the content of depression itself.

This anomaly might be eased somewhat if we could first free ourselves of the idea of depression as a discrete entity set apart from the rest of life. There exists no specific borderline over which you are "in depression" and before which you are "not in depression." It is not a separate country. And in fact many therapists are now beginning to see it as a continuum—a long line of human experience whose two poles might be loosely called "most severe depression" and "absolute absence of depression," while most of its length belongs within the realm of normality. Somewhere along the way, this continuum reaches from the normal into the abnormal.

Where along the way? That is a matter of arbitrary decision, made for research and diagnostic purposes alone. As British psychiatrists George Brown and Tirril Harris have pointed out, the "cut-off points" used to determine who is depressed and who is not, exist for no better reason than that they establish a definite field within which researchers and clinicians can work.

In fact, all such measures are necessarily provisional. Distinguishing when a badly depressed mood becomes severe depression may be as impossible, wrote Brown and Harris, "as it is to pinpoint the moment when water becomes ice." The best and the truest that can be said is that somewhere along the continuum—not at any discrete point but in a wide blurred area starting perhaps four fifths of the way up—it reaches beyond the normal into the severe.

Trying to determine exactly where we stand on this continuum at any particular time—trying to see whether we are "more" or "less" depressed, or exactly how depressed we are—is no help at all, and may even be counterproductive. The concern with classifying and measuring ourselves against an abstract and artificial standard often only makes depression more difficult to bear. The fact is that each of us fluctuates on the continuum. So long as we remain within the vast range of normality, the only really helpful question is not how depressed we are, but how well we deal with our depression—how capable we are of tolerating it and of coming through it at least a little wiser and a little stronger than before.

If we were better acquainted with those who have been severely depressed, we might be easier on ourselves. These are the people for whom depression does not pass by itself, or does so only after many months in which it settles in so deeply that is prevents routine everyday functioning, and clamps down with a relentless grip.

Carla Katznelson, for instance, battled severe depression for years, and now seems to have come through the other side of it. She has resumed full-time work as a real-estate agent, is successful and wealthy, and though not particularly happy, is no longer severely depressed. That longing for happiness, she acknowledges, played a large part in her depression: "I was always battling against myself. I remember how my mother always used to tell me 'Smile and the whole world smiles with you, cry and you cry alone,' and this sort of thing, you know, like 'You're never going to have friends if you're unhappy.' And after years of hearing that all the time, I was afraid to let it show when I was depressed. So I just tried to cut the feeling off all together. I thought maybe if I could act happy despite what I was feeling, I could convince *myself* that I was happy, as well as others. But when I tried to cut off the feeling, that's when the really severe depression began. That's when I started going down and couldn't find my way out again. I was in the pits, in the absolute dark. But now what happens. . . ." She thinks a moment, stroking the velvet on the cushions of her sofa and staring into it as though it would tell her what to say. "Now I still get low, but it's not all the way down to the bottom, and I can feel what's happening to me. It's very different. I take it as a sign to just take things easy for a while, to stop being so hard on myself. There isn't that panic that there was, and not that terrible absence of any feeling at all."

Ed Larson knows that state very well too. He lost a good job in advertising during a two-year struggle with severe depression after his divorce, and it has taken him another two years to reestablish himself in his field. Now he looks back at what happened to him with a certain awe. "Of course I still get depressed," he says, "but there's a world of difference. You can't really know it until you've experienced it, I think. However depressed I get now, I know I'll never be severely depressed like that again. I couldn't stand it, and in any case I know enough now not to let it happen. So sure, I still get depressed, but it's like night and day. The severe depression was night, and nowadays it's day: a cloudy day and lousy weather sometimes, true, but still day."

How long night and day last is often posited as an easy means of differentiating between normal and severe depression. Too easy, in fact, and too divorced from the realities and complexities of human life. Two major diagnostic scales agree on a limit of two weeks, but from very different points of view: where the one defines at least two weeks of a certain number of symptoms as a "major depressive episode," the other defines *up to* two weeks of the same symptoms as "minor depression." That would presumably leave a lot of people hanging on the cliff edge of the stroke of midnight on the fourteenth day, wondering if they are "major" or "minor."

It is pointless to determine two weeks or two months, or any specific time limit, without taking into account the circumstances of a person's life at the time. Like the cut-off point on the continuum of depression, it is an arbitrary decision. But how then are we to differentiate between severe and normal depression?

Measuring the Unmeasurable

Perhaps because we are all drawn to extremes as dramatic reflections of our own lives, the incidence of severe depression has attracted much media attention. Often only the highest figure is used as being more "newsworthy," so that a report may start by saying that ten million to twenty million Americans suffer from severe depression, and thereafter use only the figure of twenty million, automatically doubling the ante on the sole basis that the higher figure makes it more important, in the same way that a double murder gets more play on the local news that a "single" one.

Yet one can sympathize with reporters who might ask "What *is* the true figure for severe depression?" In fact, since clinical depression is defined by the fact of treatment rather than by severity, there may be no true figure.

The National Institute of Mental Health—known in the trade as "the Pentagon of mental health"—estimates in one report that eight million people a year are treated for depression, a quarter million of them in hospitals. But in another report, the NIMH states that 15 percent of the population—upward of thirty million people—suffer from clinical depression. "My God," said a friend to whom I told these figures, "if the experts don't know for sure, then who does?"

The NIMH is a vast sprawling complex in which so much research is going on, for so many different purposes, that contradictions within data are more the norm than the exception. The problem is that defining when someone is depressed is inevitably a matter of judgment, not fact. Yet there is a lot of pressure on researchers to make it appear fact.

At one time, for instance, Congress was demanding hard proof that psychotherapy is effective in treating depression before agreeing to finance treatment under Medicare. In such a situation, a clear definition of depression was a prerequisite. Congress would have no patience either with the complexity of depression or with the wide variety of schools of psychotherapy, many of which depend more on the personality and art of the therapist than on the approach used (giving rise to a situation that NIMH research head Dr. Morris Parloff describes as a "dogma eat dogma" attitude among his colleagues, each trying to prove their brand of therapy better than others and thereby reducing the complexity of human emotions and experience to the level of headaches in Anacin commercials).

Depression is not a simple matter of black and white, of "Yes, I am depressed" and "No, now I am not depressed." But researchers needing funding or proof of therapeutic efficacy need definite categories to make their points. Thus one senior researcher says that he simply doesn't trust any of the figures on depression. "When an institution puts out figures," he says, "it depends on for what purpose. If it's for funding, then obviously the figures are going to be higher. The more you can demonstrate that a problem exists, the more funding you'll get to deal with it."

Rollo May once commented somewhat archly that "the odd belief prevails in our culture that a thing or experience is not real if we cannot make it mathematical, and somehow it must be real if we can reduce it to numbers. But this means making an abstraction out of it." In the rush for statistical proof on depression, it too has been abstracted.

When "clinical depression" includes both severe depression with a strong possibility of suicide and an acute bout of normal depression where the person has sought help to alleviate the pain, the idea of depression has been abstracted beyond the point of relevance.

However, most theories of depression do break it down into some form of differentiation between severe depression and the kind most of us know. Usually, these breakdowns take the form of convenient pairings. The first half of each pair is generally easily treated with psychotherapy and will pass by itself even without clinical intervention, while the second half is a far tougher proposition, often requiring biochemical intervention with drugs, and can last for months at a time.

Some of these pairings are mild/severe, neurotic/psychotic, acute/chronic, reactive/endogenous, situational/characterological, minor/major, mood/illness, anaclitic/introspective, symptoms/syndrome. Many of them sound quite scientifically respectable, but do not mean very much. For instance, researcher

Gerald Klerman systematically sorted out the multiple criteria for differentiating between neurotic and psychotic depression, and eventually had to conclude that the term "neurotic depression" was of little value—there was only a very modest overlap between the various definitions of it. Everybody meant something else by it, thus leading us into an Alice in Wonderland situation ("You should say what you mean," the March Hare tells Alice, to which she hastily replies: "I do, at least I mean what I say—that's the same thing, you know").

Perhaps the saddest of these definitive pairings is the "unipolar/bipolar" one. In plain language, that should mean depression/manic-depression. Only it doesn't: one of the strangest statistics in psychiatry is that 68 percent to 85 percent of all manic-depressives have never been manic.

When I first read that, I thought there must have been a mistake—a careless editor or proofreader, perhaps. I went back to the source and checked, and found that there was none. Because of the intricate folkways of psychiatric diagnostic classification, there is actually such a thing as unipolar manic-depression.

Now, plain common sense tells us that this is a contradiction in terms. Bipolar means that you veer between two poles (manic and depressive), and unipolar that you are only at one pole (always depressive). Thus someone can apparently have manic-depression without the mania; since by all accounts the manic phase is great fun as long as it lasts, this sounds like some particularly unjust fate determined by vengeful Greek gods.

In bipolar manic-depression, psychiatry has focused on the depressive pole, so that it is usually only identified when severe depression sets in. In fact, the manic phase often passes for extreme affability or liveliness, and only arouses concern at the extreme, when the person concerned commits such "antisocial" acts as giving away all their money. As one expert put it, "the borderline between the successful American and the milder hypomanic patient is so elastic that the diagnosis must be made retrospectively—dependent on the success or failure of the person's behavior." Does this then mean that you are manic-depressive only if you fail, or that there might be such a thing as "successful" manic-depression which does not require treatment?

Another pairing revealed as problematic by detailed research is the "symptoms/syndrome" one. When do symptoms add up to a depressive syndrome? An NIMH team led by Jeffrey Boyd and Myrna Weissman of the Yale School of Medicine's Depression Unit compared self-rating scales for depression (where people fill in a questionnaire by themselves) to the two main epidemiological scales used for determining the degree of depression in the population (in which researchers ask the questions and check off the answers). They found only a slight relationship between the answers on the two types of scale. Someone could rate themselves as very depressed, yet prove not to be depressed at all on the epidemiological scale. In fact, 9 percent to 20 percent rated themselves high enough to be called clinically depressed, while only 6 percent qualified for "depressive disorder" on the epidemiological scales.

This means that up to two thirds of those who thought they were severely depressed were probably experiencing an acute bout of normal depression. Symptoms evidently do not a syndrome make. The researchers concluded simply that "a majority of the population has one or two depressive symptoms at any given time." But this does not make us all depressives.

Judging Normality

Attempting to cut through the morass of contradictory pseudodefinitions, Myrna Weissman, the director of the Yale Depression Unit, has emphasized that "there is no clear-cut distinction between what is normal and what is pathological, but in general, depression is pathological if it is persistent and pervasive in mood, inappropriate to circumstances, and interferes with normal functioning." This is a good working definition. But it has nothing to do with statistics and everything to do with judgment.

How long has depression to last until we call it persistent and pervasive? What do we call inappropriate to circumstances? How do we judge?

In *Whose Life Is It Anyway?*, the play and movie about a quadriplegic ex-sculptor who seeks legal permission to cut off life-support systems and thus end his life, the judgment was made in court. Faced with the prospect of a lifetime of being able to move only his face and neck muscles, the sculptor was undoubtedly depressed. But if this meant that he was incapable of rational decisions, life-support systems would have to be continued despite his opposition.

"How do you distinguish clinical depression, which might preclude the ability to make informed and logical decisions, from a perfectly sane justified feeling of depression as a result of existing conditions?" the sculptor's lawyer asks of one psychiatrist who maintains that this is a case of severe depression and that therefore permission to end life-support systems cannot be granted.

"By experience," that psychiatrist replies. Yet another psychiatrist called to the stand testifies that in the light of *his* experience, the sculptor is "reacting in a perfectly rational manner to a very bad situation."

Finally the judge questions the sculptor directly. "Do you think you're suffering from depression?" he asks.

"I *am* completely paralyzed," the sculptor replies. "I think I'd be insane if I wasn't depressed."

Passionately, he pleads that in the lack of any control over his own life, he should be allowed to exercise the ultimate choice of ending it. The judge concurs, pronouncing him "depressed but not suffering from a depressive illness" and "a brave and thoughtful man in complete possession of his faculties."

Whatever one might think about the ethics of life-support systems and the possible options in such cases, playwright Brian Clark took a tough and dramatic look at the whole question of what is known as "warrantable response." When does it make sense to be depressed, and when not?

Often, we ourselves are the worst at answering that question. The most disturbing times for many people are when depression does not seem specifically related to anything that has happened. They begin to feel that there is something "really wrong" with them if they are depressed "for no good reason."

In fact, I have never yet talked to anyone who was depressed for no reason at all. There always is a reason, and that reason usually centers around some form of loss. But this may be hard to identify if it is not obvious or "concrete." It may occur in that vast area of life where meaning is as important as actual events, objects, and people. Unaccustomed to acknowledging the importance of meaning in a society where material objects and actual relationships have more significance, many of us are literally at a loss when we confront the loss of meaning.

The label of depression can serve as a means of avoiding meaning, not only on a personal level but also on a social and cultural one. For instance, George Brown and Tirril Harris's study of London working-class women found a shockingly high incidence of chronic depression. But a good number of the women concerned were either unmarried mothers or deserted wives. And as the researchers themselves implied, it seems clear that in a society where many of the women have small children, are unemployed, have no stable partner, and live in substandard housing, depression will be endemic. They do not live in such situations because they are depressed; rather, they are depressed because of their situation. They would be very odd people if they were not.

To slap the stigma of depressive illness on such women is more of a political statement than a medical or psychological one. It reflects clinicians' attitudes toward women and society more than the existence of any predetermined illness. As British psychiatrist David Ingleby pointed out, in this situation "deciding what constitutes a 'warrantable' response to one's situation is largely and unavoidably a political decision."

For all of us, depression is basically a matter of personal politics. It belongs less to the realm of statistics and psychiatry than to that of our personal systems of belief—how we are to lead our lives, by what values, and on what level. It relates to our personal morality. Yet inevitably, social morality intervenes. We live in a social climate intolerant of depression, so that the very question of whether it might be right or wrong to be depressed, healthy or unhealthy, itself feels wrong, a transgression of accepted social values. While depression can only be a matter of clinical judgment, we have imposed a whole system of moral judgment on it.

5 *Being Right*

> I should really *like* to think that there's
>   something wrong with me—
> Because, if there isn't, then there's something
>   wrong,
> Or at least, very different from what it seemed
>   to be,
> With the world itself—and that's much more
>   frightening!
> That would be terrible. So I'd rather believe
> There is something wrong with me, that could
>   be put right.
>
> Celia to Sir Henry, in T. S. Eliot's
> *The Cocktail Party*

A couple of summers ago, a friend persuaded me to play the state lottery. She had won small prizes twice in a row, and was convinced that the lottery was a paying proposition. After being fed glass after glass of good red wine for a whole evening, I too was convinced. I went to buy a ticket the next day. On the back of the ticket, the odds of winning were printed. I read them. This certainly did not look like a paying proposition. But still buoyed up by my friend's pep talk of the night before—and slightly hung over so that the small printed details were much easier to ignore—I filled in four boxes and waited eagerly for Saturday night, when I would become a millionaire.

On Sunday morning, I figured out that if they had a prize for being farthest from winning, I would have won that prize. My friend called. She too had won nothing. "Buy again," she counseled. "You have to have persistence. I know someone who won ten thousand dollars, and she'd only been buying the lottery for two years."

Only? It seemed to me a long time to wait. Still, I bought tickets again, waited again . . . and lost again. "No, you didn't lose," my friend said. "You just didn't win, that's all." But it was hard for me to see it that way. So far as I was concerned I'd just lost another two dollars. "Look at it this way," she said, "you're buying hope for another week for just two dollars."

I tried looking at it that way and bought tickets again. I kept it up for five weeks. By the sixth week, I gave up. I just couldn't stand the idea of losing every week. "You're seeing it all wrong," my friend said. "But the chances of my winning are so minimal," I said; "just read them, they're on the back of the ticket, clearly printed." "That's not the point," she said.

The point was that I was being far too clearheaded about this whole matter. Faced with the objective chances in black on white, I could not persuade myself that my chances were any better. I was seeing things too clearly.

Being right is rarely a comfortable feeling. It leaves no room for illusion. And illusion may play a far more important role in the complex business of getting through life than we have given it credit for. My friend, for instance, still plays the lottery. To nobody's surprise except her own, she still hasn't won. But she continues to play in the obstinate optimism that some day, she will. The illusion works for her, and maybe after all she's right: to buy hope for two dollars a week is not such a bad bargain.

Her conviction that I was "seeing it all wrong" reminded me of the story of a college lecturer who went for help to a practitioner of "cognitive therapy," which works on the assumption that we are depressed simply because we are seeing things "wrong." He was depressed because when he lectured, students in his class seemed to be nodding off into sleep. He was convinced that he was a very boring lecturer, and of course this depressed him.

His therapy consisted of persuading him that what he saw was in fact not so. He was only depressed because he was convincing himself that students were going to sleep in his class; in fact, if he could just persuade himself that they were not, he would have no reason left to be depressed. For the lecturer, it worked. He emerged from therapy convinced that he was a brilliant teacher and resolved to imagine that what he had previously seen as students going to sleep was in fact students sunk in the deepest concentration. So far as he was concerned, the therapy was a complete success. But what about the students?

The therapist did not seem to give a moment's thought to the idea that maybe this man *was* a boring lecturer, maybe his students *were* going to sleep, and maybe the students were right to do this. The whole therapy was based on ignoring a certain objective reality. Just as my friend could win the lottery if she ignored the printed statistical evidence against it, so could this man be a brilliant lecturer if he just ignored his students.

The "cognitive" theory of depression is based on the work of Aaron Beck of the University of Pennsylvania, who maintains that when we are depressed, our perceptions of ourselves, of our future, and of the world around us are all distorted. We are "seeing wrong." Correct this distortion so that we "see right," and there will be no depression left.

The very assumption that we can see things "wrong" is in itself interesting. How do we establish who sees the world right, and who wrong? A Democrat believes that he sees the world right; so does a Republican. So does a religious devotee, and so does an atheist. Our attribution of rightness and wrongness to their perceptions depends solely on what we ourselves think or would like to think. Yet the "cognitive" approach advocated by Professor Beck assumes absolute standards for thought and perception.

I doubt that Beck would argue that beauty is absolute instead of in the proverbial eye of the beholder, or that he would argue for absolute truth in modern science, when physics is the giddy history of one paradigm rapidly replacing another, challenging the conventions that we previously took for granted. Yet he does exactly this for depression.

Since depression is merely a matter of distorted perception, he argues, all that is needed is to readjust perception and the depression will disappear. It is all a matter of seeing things differently. The only thing "wrong" in the first place was the unaccountable insistence on the part of the depressed person on seeing things the wrong way.

The trouble is that this is little more than a

scientized "power of positive thinking." It gets results, of course—a high "cure" rate with dramatic and obvious improvement, partly because the results are often measured by a scale developed by Beck himself, and partly because it has been used mainly with severely depressed people. Yet it pays no attention at all to the reasons why someone might be depressed. In fact, it denies that there is any reason beyond distorted perception. It treats only the symptoms of depression—the way people see things when they are depressed. And in doing so, it is based on a fundamentally incorrect assumption. In fact, when we are depressed, we may see things far more objectively and with far less distortion and illusion than usual.

Sadder but Wiser?

In 1979, two research psychologists, Lauren Alloy of Northwestern University and Lyn Abramson of the State University of New York at Stony Brook, did a series of experiments on students to gauge whether depressed people did indeed have distorted perceptions. They found that far from having a distorted view of the world, those who are depressed judge reality far better than those who are not.

As such experiments must be, the setup was carefully planned to produce results that depended as little as possible on the judgment of the researchers. To the nonpsychologist, it will doubtless sound somewhat Pavlovian. Both depressed and nondepressed students were asked to switch on various colored lights by pressing different buttons. Though the students did not know it, the lights were fixed. For one group, various colored lights would come on no matter which button they pressed; they had only minimal control. Other groups had increasing amounts of control, so that there was far more correspondence between what button they pressed and which light came on. After some time at the light console, the students were then asked to estimate how much control they thought they had.

Depressed and nondepressed students judged the situation very differently. Nondepressed students exaggerated the situation, whatever it was: when they had a lot of real control (75 percent), they overestimated their power; when they had little control (25 percent), they underestimated it, feeling more helpless than they really were. Yet in both instances, depressed students assessed their degree of control quite accurately. They thought themselves neither more powerful nor more helpless than they really were.

The students were then offered an extra quarter for each time they produced a green light on the console. In fact, there was now no relation at all between which button they pressed and when the green light came on. Nevertheless, nondepressed students believed they had some control of the situation; they abandoned rational strategy for intuition, creating an illusion of control where there was none. (Players of the lottery or of the British football pools do much the same thing when they fill in their tickets according to "magic" numbers such as anniversaries, ages, house numbers, and so on.) Depressed students were far more likely to work the situation out rationally and behave accordingly, pressing buttons at random.

Intrigued by what happened when money was involved, the researchers now arranged matters so that students could lose as well as win money by playing the console, meanwhile fixing the failure-success rate at exactly fifty-fifty. They found that when they lost money by playing, nondepressed students overestimated their failure rate, while depressed students recalled it accurately; conversely, when they won money, nondepressed students overestimated their success—and depressed students were once again accurate.

It was clear that those subject to "cognitive illusions" were not the depressed students but the nondepressed ones. Alloy and Abramson thus raised the age-old question: Were depressed people not "sadder but wiser" than others? "A crucial question," they concluded, "is whether depression itself leads people to be 'realistic' or whether realistic people are more vulnerable to depression."

A crucial question, certainly, and a painful one. If people have the illusion of control when they are not depressed, then depression must be seen as the loss of that illusion, as well as all manner of other illusions by which we make it easier for ourselves to exist in a world little given to individual control.

Aaron Beck's approach to depression assumes that far more control is possible; his "wrong thinkers" live in delusion as he sees it—and this may be *his* illusion. Yet his strange combination of behavioral and analytic techniques has attracted much attention and funding. One primary reason may be that none of us cares to admit how little control we might really have over our own world. To see things too clearly may be terrifying. Better illusion than clarity.

The Problem of Awareness

To be too aware can make living very difficult. When we are depressed, we see too much—too much suffering and unhappiness, too much difficulty and struggle. The defenses we usually maintain for filtering out these perceptions are down. A different and terrifying order of reality appears.

This is what is expressed by the character Bernard in the closing section of Virginia Woolf's novel *The Waves*: "I observed with disillusioned clarity the despicable nonentity of the street; its porches; its window curtains; the drab clothes, the cupidity and complacency of shopping women; and old men taking the air in comforters; the caution of people crossing; the universal determination to go on living, when really, fools and gulls that you are, I said, any slate may fly from a roof, any car may swerve. . . . With dispassionate despair, with entire disillusionment, I surveyed the dust dance. . . . How can I proceed now, I said, without a self, weightless and visionless, through a world weightless, without illusion?"

Most psychotherapies have assumed that awareness can only be good, and that the more a person can see the world without illusion, the more rational and sane that person will be. But the loss of illusion can be seen in quite a different way: as a tragic loss of meaning leading to a perception of the world that is too unsparing and too bleak for any human being to withstand without despair. Consequently, theorists have been well aware of the limits of awareness since the very beginning of psychology.

Sigmund Freud noted that many of those whom he called "melancholic" were quite justified in the way they saw the world; such people had "a keener eye for the truth than other people who are not melancholic," he wrote. But then he introduced a nasty Catch-22: even if the depressed person was seeing the world truly and clearly, he had to be ill since no healthy person would dream of talking of themselves in such dire terms. "We only wonder why a man has to be ill before he can be accessible to a truth of this kind," Freud wrote, since "it may be, so far as we know, that he has come pretty near to understanding himself."

It is a stunning tautology: if you are depressed then you must be sick, since if you were healthy you could not possibly see yourself with such penetrating clarity and understanding. It is as though Freud were saying, "Yes, you are right," and then in the same breath, "But that makes you wrong."

How can "a keener eye for the truth" be wrong? That depends, it seems, on the dimensions of the truth: not on the degree to which one is correct, but on the moral sense of right or wrong.

Many philosophers have seen depression as ultimately right. Aristotle called it "the gist of genius." Kant saw the depressed person as an almost mythic paragon of "true virtue." For Kierkegaard, depression was the experience of "authentic consciousness," something which differentiated an enlightened and imaginative elite from what he called the mass of "the Philistines." And Roman Guardini called it "an experience in which the critical point of our human condition becomes clear" and "a journey from the superficial to the mystery of origins."

Mystics have willingly gone into the deepest depression in search of a near-sublime affirmation of truth; romantics have seen it as the highest state of human perception. Yet there is something inhuman in this view of the depressed person as a kind of tragically defined *Übermensch* who has reached exalted depths beyond the ken of the majority. The fact remains that any normal perception of "inner truth" has more of the bleakness of Virginia Woolf's Bernard than of some mystical intimation. The light of depression is gray, not blindingly bright. There is no comfort in being right, no honor in seeing without illusion. There is not even the consolation of any ultimate clarity. As Ortega y Gasset argued, it may well be that "life is at the start a chaos in which one is lost. The individual suspects this, but he is frightened at finding himself face to face with this terrible reality, and tries to cover it over with a curtain of fantasy."

Usually, the curtain can be drawn. We manage to persuade ourselves that we know what we are doing, that we are in control, that our lives are meaningful and worthwhile and secure—until something happens that rips the curtain away and shakes up everything we took for granted.

The Loss of Illusion

Taking things for granted is often essential. If we couldn't take most things for granted, we would never be able to get anything done. We need the obvious, in that we need to accept our own values and be able to act on them without being constantly aware of them.

But R. D. Laing once noted that "the obvious is literally that which stands in one's way." There are times when we take too much for granted. At such times, losing the obvious can open up the way, allowing us to question ourselves.

On a permanent basis, of course, constant questioning of our beliefs and assumptions would make life impossible. Every one of us would become a Hamlet, lacking the basic confidence to move out into the world and to act in it. But we do need times of questioning, even if we have to be forced into them by circumstance, so that we can shake out any cobwebs that threaten to bind our values into a rigid and inflexible web.

Such times are inevitably those of depression. As Herman Hesse described it in *Steppenwolf*, "Every occasion when a mask was torn off, an ideal broken, was preceded by this hateful vacancy and stillness, this deathly constriction and loneliness and unrelatedness, this waste and empty hell of lovelessness and despair."

When the broken ideal is central to your life, the loss of illusion can be resisted for years—making the final unmasking even more shattering. Lionel

Carson, for instance, found this out when he lost his faith in Communism. Until the midfifties, he had managed to rationalize the growing evidence of Stalinism, and clung to the conviction that this was just an aberration and that the revolution would be righted. Like most political dogmatists, he was convinced that he was right, that he and his friends had the answer to the human dilemma, and that those who did not realize this might have to be forced into it a little for their own good.

Then came the Hungarian uprising of 1956 and its ruthless repression by the Soviets. Lionel was shaken, but could not renounce Communism immediately. It takes far longer than that to make such a basic change in one's life. Instead, he now recalls, "It seems like I lived in a state of low-grade depression for two whole years. I thought I'd found the answer, and then the answer was revealed as just as bad as any other answer. And if this wasn't the answer, then what was? Was there any answer at all? For years, ever since I'd been a student, my whole life had revolved around this ideal. And now, if I was to let it go, there'd be nothing there at all, nothing to take its place, nothing to believe in." He shrugs and smiles half-mockingly, pushing his glasses up over his forehead. "I suppose I needed very badly to believe. But then we all do, don't we?"

At first, he felt that he had failed the faith, and only slowly realized that instead, his faith had failed him. "It was easier somehow to blame myself," he says, "because then at least the ideal still stood firm. It was just me that was shaky. I didn't have the right outlook, and that was my problem, not a problem with Communism itself. And then I suppose I couldn't face the whole changeover in my life that would take place—that did take place—when I left the party. I lost my friends, my wife, everything changed. It's funny you know, but even now, looking back, it seems that things were far simpler then, when I had faith, and still believed in it all. I know this sounds odd now, but they were innocent times. It was an illusion, true, but we were happy in that illusion. That's something, isn't it?"

Living without illusion—without a sense of meaning in what many philosophers see as an essentially meaningless world—is impossible on a long-term basis. We all construct our own meanings, our own systems of values, and base our lives on them. Yet most of us remain barely aware of them. Striving for meaning, we avoid thinking about it too much, as though the very fact of considering it threatened to dissolve it.

Usually, we enjoy the illusion of being meaningful, of being secure, of being able to rely on our world. We arrange our lives so that a certain amount of routine and predictability will keep the wolf of vulnerability from the door. We know the wolf is there, but we ignore it if we can. We may take an intellectual pleasure in Greek dramas or in Pinter or Beckett plays, where the characters struggle against fate or absurdity or their own isolation, but we do not really think of ourselves in that same way. Not until we are depressed. Until we are forced into disillusionment.

A loss of illusion underlies much depression. Like the depressed students who assessed their effectiveness more accurately than others, we see with a bleak objectivity. If anyone wants to feel a warm sense of inner value and basic security, maintained Ernest Becker, that person "has to repress globally, from the entire spectrum of his experience." When the repression no longer succeeds, we are left without defenses in what seems to be a hostile world. We feel bereft of an illusion that formerly sustained us.

One of the most sustaining illusions of modern life is that of the perfect love relationship—the grail of so many people's lives, sometimes repeatedly found and lost. Many of us enter into marriage or a relationship with the starry-eyed belief that we have found the perfect partner and will have the ideal relationship. This is how Ira Garvey felt when he moved in with his girlfriend; two years later, when they broke up, he became deeply depressed—even though he had welcomed the breakup.

"I don't understand it," he said despondently. "It doesn't make sense. I know I'm glad we've finished. I'm sorry about all the pain we caused each other, and I'm sorry we both had to go through all that, deeply sorry, but on the other hand it was clear that we were just making each other miserable, that we just couldn't live together. So why do I feel depressed now? I mean, surely I should be feeling happier than I was, not unhappier?"

What Ira had failed to take into account was that he had lost not only his relationship but also his ideal of love and companionship, and his idea of himself as a mature partner capable of living that ideal. He had to face the possibility that what had seemed ideal at the very beginning might itself have been an illusion. Could he love again? Was he capable of it?

Struggling to answer those questions, Ira had to overcome a new sense of futility in love, and work through to a willingness to be open to it again—and thus to be vulnerable to hurt again. Subconsciously, he was tempted by the position of cartoonist Jules Feiffer's young professional man, whose expression is alternately hopeful and depressed as he declares: "I open myself to love. I get hurt. I close myself to love. I get lonely. I reopen myself to love. I get clobbered. I close myself to love. I get depressed. I reopen myself to love. I get destroyed. I close myself to love. I self-destruct. I open myself to despair. [And with a big grin:] Safe."

Endings leave one feeling adrift somehow, vulnerable to the future. They are rarely as "tidy" as we would like them to be. What comes to an end is not only the relationship itself, but also the ideal of how it should have been. Faith in that ideal is shattered; expectations have been betrayed by reality.

A. Alvarez wrote of his first marriage that "the expectations which I had brought to the marriage were disproportionate to a degree which was more or less inhuman. The sense of failure which followed almost instantaneously was equally disproportionate and left no room for qualities that might have saved us: patience, tolerance, a sense of humor. . . . I felt like a priest who has failed his faith."

When this happens, reality is found wanting. Worse, our own selves are found wanting beside the glitter of the ideal. Though the glitter has faded, our eagerness to maintain it forever—our own faith in it—makes us see only darkness by comparison, as though someone had suddenly flicked the switch in a lighted room.

The Alvarez marriage had been consciously patterned, on his side at least, on a literary model—that of D. H. and Frieda Lawrence. Thus it was doomed from the start, not being his own, but someone else's. It seems absurd that anyone should try to base a marriage on such a premise, yet we are all tempted to pattern our close relationships after one model or another: the marriages of parents or of friends who seem happy enough, the marriages we see depicted in movies or on television, the legendary marriages of fiction or of popular renown. Presidential marriages are held up as role models—at least until after the presidents concerned have died. Jean-Paul Sartre and Simone de Beauvoir were the models for numerous unmarried relationships in the fifties and sixties, when "living together" was not accepted as it is now. Elizabeth Taylor and Richard Burton have even carved out a special niche for themselves as antimodels—how *not* to do it.

Given the variety of such models, it is amazing how consistent the ideal of a good marriage remains. The core of the ideal has held. Despite the fact that nearly one out of every two American marriages ends in divorce, Americans continue to marry in the good faith that they will be in the nondivorced half of the population. Nearly half of them are then faced with the struggle through disillusionment.

Very often, it seems easier to blame oneself than to blame the illusion. Unable to let go of the picture of the ideal marriage, many divorcing people accuse themselves of being somehow lacking, of being unable to live up to the ideal and therefore at fault. Thus the terrible expression "a failed marriage," as though marriage could be graded for "pass" and "fail" or assessed on the now infamous scale up to ten.

Perhaps we simply expect too much perfection. If we could plan instead for imperfection, perfection might arrive by chance, unburdened by expectations and preconceptions. The fixed ideal of the perfect marriage or relationship is as unreal as any other inspirational ideal. It pretends that it is possible to ignore the inevitable tensions of two people living together and building both their individual and their shared lives simultaneously. There is little acknowledgment that such tensions are part of marriage, and that grappling with them is essential to the maturation of a marriage. Such ideals, in short, make us look forward to something inherently false, and undermine reality. They set us up for disillusionment.

The Nuclear Illusion

So long as our ideals are based on a personal sense of values, we can handle the depression that comes if they are revealed as illusions. The values which led us to that ideal still exist; though they have been challenged by disillusionment, they will survive all the better for being held up to the light of day, examined, and eventually reaffirmed. Despite the feeling of hopelessness, we are not in complete despair about the future. We have an acute awareness that our hopes have not been fulfilled, and may not ever be, but this does not preclude all hope altogether, as does despair.

In fact, depression is almost an expression of faith in the future; there should be and can be hope, one feels, if only one can find the way to it. The feeling of "I can't" so common in depression is not so much the failure of belief that there can be a future, as the temporary inability to create one in the imagination, a new "promised land" of desires, wishes, and hopes that will transcend emptiness, futility, and apathy.

When the loss of illusion threatens all our values, however, depression becomes almost intolerable. It challenges everything we live for, the most basic assumptions by which we lead our lives. A world without values is a world without meaning, and in this world, depression itself loses all meaning. It is replaced by numbing.

This is clearest, perhaps, in the mass degree of psychic numbing with regard to the threat of nuclear destruction. It seems so mind-boggling, so overwhelming, that we have invented numerous ways to cling to the illusion that we can and will survive, no matter what.

Quite recently, in fact, as I was preparing an article on the spread of nuclear weapons to formerly "nonnuclear" countries, I came across one of those maps that show what would happen if a one-megaton nuclear bomb were to hit Manhattan, falling on Times Square. The map showed concentric circles of damage; the circle of instantaneous death reached just short of where I was living at the time. My first reaction, automatic, was "Oh, good, I'll be all right." My second reaction was "Did I really think that?"

I could hardly believe my own first reaction. I had marched in the first Aldermaston antinuclear marches in England over twenty years before, and had long been awesomely acquainted with the details of what happens to the immediate survivors of a nuclear explosion. My desk was full of reports and papers on nuclear destruction and the spread of nuclear weapons. Yet still, something in me resisted what I knew. I too still clung to the illusion that I could survive. Others would die, not me.

Even thinking about this whole issue is so threatening that until recently it was practically avoided in the United States. The sense of radical insecurity that it provokes was simply too much to confront and acknowledge. As psychiatrist Robert Jay Lifton has put it, "the idea of *any* human future becomes a matter of profound doubt. In that image, we or perhaps our children are the last human beings. There is no one after us to leave anything to. We become cut off, collectively self-enclosed, something on the order of a vast remnant. . . . If we lose our sense of future, we question our past."

When faith in the future is broken, we go beyond depression, into despair. If large-scale nuclear destruction is possible, there may *be* no "promised land" anywhere in the future; there may be no future at all. The past becomes utterly meaningless, whatever it contained. The idea that there might be not only nothing for you, personally, but nothing at all, for anyone, threatens the most basic assumptions of society, culture, and human existence.

The fact that most people feel they have absolutely no control over the spread and buildup of nuclear weapons makes them feel all the more vulnerable and helpless. Denial and clinging to the illusion of survival become understandable yet self-destructive responses. They provide a shelter from despair, yet at the possible price of personal survival.

If one does consider the nuclear threat, one is brought up short against a concept of individual human life as expendable, of oneself as just one of millions who would die, part of the "acceptable casualties." Any possible sense of meaning in death is thus eliminated—and with it, any sense of meaning in life too. Psychic numbing—ignoring the threat, "rationalizing" it, even joking about it—is a means of surviving the threat of nonsurvival. But as Lifton cogently argues, such a state is highly pathological; it denies reality and achieves the very opposite of its own aim.

Depression is the only sane reaction. In fact there are now many antinuclear organizations around the country that run special counseling groups for those who, having surrendered illusion, are depressed. Only by working through the depression, they maintain, can the person find the determination and incentive to work toward nuclear arms reduction and eventual disarmament.

Even when awareness is allowed to hit, a certain distancing still often takes place. Talking about the nuclear situation, people tend to say "It is depressing" rather than "I am depressed," as though the depression belonged to a plane of worldly affairs that does not really impinge on personal security. The threat to the sense of continuity seems to be too radical, the rationale for nuclear deterrence too chancy, to be translated directly into personal terms.

Psychiatrists now talk about "therapeutic depression"—a stage in the emergence of the schizophrenic from complete withdrawal. This stage, they say, is welcome, since it marks a return of feeling and emotion; it is a clear sign that the schizophrenic is beginning to return to the world of others. In the same way, depression about the nuclear threat marks the return of feeling and awareness—the emergence from psychic numbing. It means that the person is finally facing the facts.

Confronting a threat is the essential prelude to attempting to do something about it. So long as we ignore, deny, or repress the threat, there is nothing we can do to stop it. Overwhelmed by helplessness, we make that feeling into fact by numbing ourselves. We preserve the illusion of invulnerability when only the loss of that illusion and the consequent depression can be considered sane and productive. While numbing only reinforces the spiral of possible nothingness, depression is essential: without it, we go blindly forward into the despair of what may be no future at all.

6 Being Lost

> She had lost all our memories for ever, and it was
> as though by dying she had robbed me of part of
> myself. I was losing my individuality. It was the
> first stage of my own death, the memories drop-
> ping off like gangrened limbs.
>
> GRAHAM GREENE, *The End of the Affair*

Identity is not created in isolation. The pattern of ex-
perience and wished-for experience lends meaning
and texture to the present, giving us a clear feeling
of who we are. It establishes continuity and, through
that, a sense of control. We have at least the illusion
that we are not prey to the whims of fate or of an
uncaring God—that we have some power to shape
our lives.

Loss and change challenge this, requiring us to
rethread the strand of coherently related events. We
feel endangered, as though all the work of our identity were being subverted by chance or circumstance. At such times, we are forced into redefining
ourselves.

Often, this redefinition is a minor one. But sometimes, especially with changes in personal status, it

can be quite major. The transition from single to married, or from married to widowed or divorced, is a major change in identity. So is the transition from child to adolescent and from adolescent to adult. These are the times when we have to think twice when filling in "personal status" sections on application forms, for instance, just as we hesitate over what date to write on a check in the first month of a new year. What becomes automatic with time requires conscious thought at first; we cannot take it for granted. A major part of ourselves seems strange to us. We are not quite at home in our new selves. Something is missing.

Depression always involves a loss, and that threatens identity. Facing loss, we feel lost. If you are in the middle of change and reorganization, if your life has been disrupted in some way, if your world has crumbled or the carpet has been pulled out from under you—if everything that seems worth living for is suddenly in question or lost or hidden by the shock of the new—you are pulled up short. You are stopped, as it were, in the track of life. The thread of continuity has snapped.

It was never that smooth to begin with, of course. The thread of each of our lives is less one smooth continuum than a well-worn and almost ragged line, full of knots where frayed ends have been clumsily tied together as though some nervous child had been playing with it. At times, there seems no purpose to all these knots; the thread seems to lead nowhere. Sometimes it can be as vague yet pervasive a feeling as a loss of direction.

Recently, for example, Liz Prentice felt oddly confused and depressed. She had what seemed to be almost a glamorous life—a filmmaker husband, the looks of a *Vogue* model, two blond and beautiful children, and an airy sunlit apartment overlooking Manhattan's Central Park, full of books and artwork. But while her husband's career had become highly successful, Liz felt left behind. She had organized a successful arts festival some months before, but then for a long time had not known what to do next. Finally she had taken a job as a fund-raiser for the arts, but it was a new post, created especially for her, and she felt that it was too amorphous, unclear in its aims.

"That's the trouble," she explained, digging at the rind of a grapefruit as we sat over the breakfast table. "There's nothing concrete to it, and I don't know where I'm going. The whole thing makes me feel lost. I get very depressed about it, and I think this depression is really from confronting that void of not knowing where I'm going."

She sighed, pushing the grapefruit away. "I suppose, too, it's that I'm afraid—afraid of taking an important step forward, of carving this job out for myself. It's hard and scary, and risky too in a way—if I fail, I mean. I know I should do it, but I don't really see any purpose to it. Why put myself through all this? So I just sit here and get depressed instead. . . . I feel sort of cut adrift, like nothing really has any meaning."

Without a sure sense of shape, meaning, and direction, she was at a loss. Forced into an unwelcome questioning of the basis on which she was living her life, she was faced with the onerous task of reshaping it into purpose and meaning. But meanwhile, shaken free of any firm identity, she looked at herself and at her life with a jaundiced eye.

Usually, we all conceive of ourselves as bigger, in some way, than we really are. Love and hope, faith and expectation, security and meaning all combine to give us a sense of well-being, or at least a sense that there is some point in our existence. We do not live in "the" world, but in the world that each of us creates. The sense of "I" comes from this world. The feeling of being oneself, unique and important, depends on cutting out the awareness of the real size of the world and our minute place in it. We never quite outgrow the childlike sense that the world revolves around us, or that our own individual world *is* "the" world.

Loss challenges this conviction with sometimes sudden force. In the absence of meaning, it is hard to imagine future meaning. In depression, we mourn the loss of someone or something that gave meaning to our lives. And we search for a replacement. But new meaning is built on the loss of the old; before we can build it, then, we face the painful task of absorbing the many levels of loss, tangible and intangible, that we are prey to.

That is far easier said than done. How do we come to terms with loss without rejecting the person or quality that has been lost and, in so doing, rejecting that part of ourselves that found meaning in them? It becomes almost a question of loyalty to the past. The very idea of life without a loved person who has died or left you seems disloyal to that person. And the very idea of life without a previously treasured ideal seems disloyal to one's own self, since when the loss is intangible—not a person or a thing but an idea, a sense, a quality of life that we took for granted but never defined—we feel that we have betrayed ourselves. Unable to pinpoint this kind of loss yet feeling the emptiness it leaves, we fear that something is "really wrong."

Loss of direction, loss of an ideal, loss of challenge, of control, of structure or of a feeling of rootedness—all these types of loss and more confront us as we move through life. They are the elements which create the texture of our lives, the warp and the woof that make up the rich and complex tapestry of each individual history. Without them, we feel empty and depressed. Yet this feeling of emptiness is an essential part of coming to terms with loss. What feels like nothingness is in fact part of a healing process.

Nothing more can grow from within unless what has already grown is parted from. We need to take our leave psychologically as well as physically. This does not necessarily mean rejection of the past; it means acceptance of separation.

Memory can be a warm presence, but the parting which transforms present into past is not sweet sorrow at all. It is like seeing a piece of yourself go. We have all experienced the sad emptiness of even the most minor parting—as we watch the plane take off, for example, or walk back down the platform after the train has pulled out (the scene so beloved of moviemakers). It is a feeling compounded of many elements—abandonment, uprootedness, something loose or unstable. But the sense of emptiness that underlies it is vitally important.

When someone is "full," there is no room for new things, new relationships, new commitments. The energy is all committed, as it were. When the basis of this commitment is taken away, whether slowly or suddenly, by your own choice or not, the emptiness that it leaves is the prerequisite for new commitment, whether of love, belief, energy, trust, loyalty or faith.

Think of plowed ground that must be left fallow for a time every few years. If you plant again too soon, the soil will be used up and impoverished. Most crops planted on such soil will be meager and stunted. The soil needs time to recover, to regain its natural nutrients. And so, in a way, do we.

There can be no fullness without emptiness, just as there can be no day without night. The biblical account of creation describes the earth as "without form and void"—*tohu ve'bohu,* meaning an anarchic disorder, a state where nothing can be relied upon and there is neither meaning nor reason. The creation was thus a process of establishing an order. Emptiness cannot be filled in anarchy, since the anarchy only feeds on emptiness, compounding it.

In our own lives, the creation of new meaning and relevance grows out of depression. Loss forces us into it. But it takes its own time; we cannot rush the process. Moreover, there is no blueprint for how it should be done. Nothing ever works out quite as it should according to the textbooks or the theories of depression. There are always echoes, always strands to be worked out later, smaller leave-takings to be made until finally, many weeks, months, or even years later, we realize that we have moved on from the past.

At the time of writing, for instance, it is four years since I moved from the Middle East to the United States—and went into a deep depression three months after the move itself. Yet however much I now think I have come to terms with it, there is always the awareness that this acceptance remains to some degree tenuous. There are still times when the past pulls achingly at the present, when I look at New York and long for Jerusalem. And this, I think, applies to all such separations. Some might call it nostalgia, but I think it is far more than that: there may simply be no perfect accommodation with the past. Even in this, we must accept imperfection.

I now realize that the depression I experienced then was basically a healing—a long, slow coming to terms with the multiple loss of love and friends, familiarity and style of life, country and involvement. Without it, I would have been living physically in one place, and psychologically in another, torn between the two—as indeed I was for a while—and unable to be completely in either. My own sense of identity—of myself being, working, and belonging in a certain place, in a certain time, with purpose and meaning in my being there—would have been entirely eroded.

All normal depression fulfills basically the same purpose: it is a process of healing from the hurt of loss, and from the painful challenge to the sense of self entailed in this loss. If we fight, deny, or repress it, we not only prolong the depression but prevent it from achieving its purpose.

127

Mourning and Melancholia

Defensively, we usually think of loss only in terms of the death of someone close to us. But in fact the varieties of human loss are immense: love, a job, familiarity or rootedness, ideals, hope or expectations, faith or trust. . . . Just as we grieve for the physical loss of someone when we mourn, so too we need to grieve for symbolic loss in depression.

To look at depression as a form of mourning may at first seem a denial of the shattering implications of death, as though the death of a husband or wife could be compared to teenage rejection in love. There is of course a major difference between a person passing out of *your* life and their passing out of life entirely. But when someone dies, you grieve not only for the person, but for yourself—for the emptiness of your own continued existence without that person. So too in depression, we grieve for the meaninglessness of our own selves without a lost love or purpose. We grieve for ourselves when meaning and satisfaction are missing, whatever the reason. And we do this not out of self-pity, but because we have to adjust to the loss of previous sources of meaning and satisfaction before we are free to find new ones.

We grieve because we feel deprived of our own identities. We are self-centered in this grief, but not necessarily in a pejorative sense; the self, after all, is the basis of our experience of the world.

When Freud first introduced the idea of "mourning work" in his essay *Mourning and Melancholia,* he contrasted the normal process of mourning with the abnormal state of severe depression. He used the word "mourning" in a far wider sense than we do nowadays; he defined it as "the reaction to the loss of a loved person, or to the loss of some abstraction which has taken the place of one, such as country, liberty, an ideal."

But country, liberty, and ideals do not necessarily "take the place of" a loved person. We can love someone very deeply and yet also be deeply committed to such "abstract" things. Basically, Freud was saying simply that we mourn not only loss by death, but also the loss of anything, material or abstract, tangible or intangible, that we feel deeply attached to or that has had particular importance in our lives.

"In mourning, the world has become poor and empty; in melancholia, it is the ego itself," Freud continued. Yet his very elegance confused the issue. "World" and "ego" are far more intricately intertwined than his phrasing allows. We all live in our own worlds—the world each of us sees, is interested in, and is involved in. Self and world are symbiotic in our system of identity and personal relevance. To use the psychoanalytic term, we "incorporate"—we assume possession, using terms like "my husband," "my country," "my ideas" or "my politics." By now it is a commonplace to say that a very insecure person will place overly great value on material possessions. But we are none of us that secure, and we all place great value on all manner of less tangible, symbolic possessions because they are part of our means of defining ourselves, of establishing where we stand vis-à-vis the world at large.

When some part of ourselves that defined us is

lost, for whatever reason, our sense of identity is severely threatened. What we had previously taken for granted is now in question. It feels as though we ourselves have become a question mark. All our energy is then drawn inward to deal with this threat, entering into the mourning to resolve that question and find a way to reconstruct identity more in tune with changed circumstances. If this work is well done, we will emerge with a renewed sense of identity and meaning.

Sociologist Peter Marris described this process well. "Recovery from grief," he wrote, "depends on restoring a sense that the lost attachment can still give meaning to the present. . . . It cannot be treated simply as a rational process of learning to make the best of things, where grief is merely to be endured. The working out of grief is itself the central, most urgent task, because the bereaved cannot repair the ability to learn any meaningful ways of coping until they have undertaken it."

This demands energy, so that it is no wonder that depressed and mourning people are exhausted. "Even when the loss is peripheral," says Marris, "the sense of disorientation, of experience being drained of part of its meaning, sets up a nagging anxiety. If this minor grief is ignored, I think it may be more upsetting, in unrecognized ways, than it need have been. Moving house, for instance, or taking a new job, may involve the sacrifice of familiar relationships with neighbors, colleagues, a community whose interest one shared, and though the new house or job may be better, that does not overcome the need to mourn, at least a little, for the loss."

Often, such disruptive changes are imposed on us. A lover may leave of his or her volition, not ours; a new job may demand that we move; we may be fired. Whenever this happens, loss is all the harder to accept because it involves a challenge to our sense of control. On top of the loss of love, place, or job, we have also lost control of our own lives. We are left with that haunting feeling of "if only"—if only we had tried harder/been younger/worked later/been more compromising/not given in so much. . . . We do not eschew responsibility for our own lives, as so many of the new "training therapies" maintain. On the contrary, in many instances we ascribe too much responsibility to ourselves.

The illusion that we control our own lives is both strengthening and weakening: strengthening in that it keeps the winds of fate well at bay (those same winds that allowed the ancient Greek dramatists to express some of the most basic human dilemmas) and weakening in that there is then the constant fear that we will lose control. This is the fear that makes acceptance of loss so hard and that makes us so resistant to change.

We cannot help but change, of course. Change is part of the dynamic of life. We grow from childhood into adolescence, leave home, graduate from college, begin a career, get married, have children, buy a home, watch the children go out into the world. . . . We move from youth into middle age, and from middle age into old age. Growth itself is change; time is change. Yet even when change is welcome, it always involves leaving something behind—youth, perhaps, or familiarity or innocence.

We feel disorganized at such times, even frightened. It is as though there were nothing to rely on, no bulwark to lean back on for support. Like Liz Prentice at the beginning of this chapter, we feel cut adrift in our new selves.

Martin Lucas felt this way, to his astonishment, shortly after he began work at the job he'd been aiming for ever since he left college, as a junior partner in a prestigious law firm. "It's not that I don't know my work," he said. "That's not the problem. But I feel . . . like I'm not quite sure what's expected of me, not sure where to put my feet. It's like I'm living in suspension for the time being, and it's very difficult. Nothing seems quite solid."

His feelings were not dissimilar from those of theologian C. S. Lewis as he described his grief after his wife's death: "Grief still feels like fear. Perhaps, more strictly, like suspense. Or like waiting; just hanging around waiting for something to happen. It gives life a permanently provisional feeling. It doesn't seem worth starting anything. I can't settle down."

Whatever the loss, we cannot look to the future until we have mourned the past. Mourning is the means by which we come to terms with change. If we evade it, we only remain bound to the past, and lose the capacity to act in and enjoy the present.

The Failure of Evasion

If we refuse to come to terms with change, we stultify; if we refuse to grieve, we become trapped by that undone grieving, victims of our own acknowledged emotion.

In the short term, it often seems easier to fight or to deny loss than to go through the painful process of reconciliation to it. Many even try to persuade themselves that if they refuse to accept loss, it never took place or is still reversible. "He still really loves me," said a young woman whose former boyfriend had just announced his plans to marry someone else. "I know it. He just feels he has to marry her, that he can't come back because of pride and so many other things. You'll see, it won't work out." They had broken up over a year before, and she still refused to accept it—and in that time, of course, had been quite unable to form any new attachment.

A certain bathos and absurdity mark those who insist on living in the present as though it were the past. The exaggerated toughness of the retired military man, the girlish style of an older woman who always depended on men for approval, the petulant selfishness of a young man who was a spoiled child—all such artifice indicates a little death of the personality, a clinging to a worn-out identity for fear of finding a present one.

The problem is partly that we no longer have rituals for mourning. We never did have them for symbolic mourning, and even those for mourning death are losing ground in a secular society. Mourning embarrasses us, and depression even more so, as though the mourning work described by Freud were not a vital and demanding process of giving up and letting go but merely a shameful waste of emotion.

"If we do not know how to mourn, we cannot know how to live," said Peter Marris, "and the diffuse strain of unacknowledged grief will destroy our liberalism and our respect for life." But how are we to know how to mourn when even at funerals, mourners are admired for how well they "bear up" and for *not* crying or breaking down?

Ironically, the traditional religions, often criticized as reactionary, do sustain this respect for life by giving status and form to grief, if only grief for death. A Catholic requiem mass gives public acknowledgment to private grief. The traditional wake brings forth emotion, tears, and memories in a time set aside to mark the dead person's passing. The Jewish *shiva* demands seven days of full-time mourning; those coming to sit with the bereaved family are forbidden to consol them in the sense of trying to cheer them up—their role is to encourage and participate in the mourning, not to alleviate it.

All mourning involves a dual process of separation and continuity. While separation must be acknowledged, continuity must also be established—what is lost must be absorbed in the memory. The point is not to forget, but to alter the personal significance from present to past, and then to retain the past as memory instead of as a haunting presence or possibility.

Whatever you may believe about ghosts, the symbolism of ghostly appearances is clear: it is not the ghost who has no rest, but those who see the ghost. Unable to put the dead person to rest in their own minds, they cling to an ethereal form of continued presence. The ghost thus becomes their own ghost—the ghost of that part of them that they feel has been lost with the dead person.

Everyone has such ghosts—parts of our selves that we never made peace with. Lost opportunities, lost youth, lost ideals, lost love—these are ethereal, intangible presences of the past. As with the ghosts of the dead, they must be laid to rest through mourning, or they will continue to haunt us.

The intricate blending of bereavement, depression, mourning, and identity comes through clearly in the story of Alice Martins, who became severely depressed after her home burned down. The only fortunate thing about that summer night, she remembers, was that the children were staying with friends. Otherwise it was a total disaster. She and her husband could only stand and watch as the flames consumed everything they owned.

"I knew that I was lucky to be alive," she remembers, "but it didn't help at all when people kept on telling me that. I could only remember watching everything go up in smoke. I know now that I began to confuse things right there, when it happened. Watching my whole past, everything we'd accumulated and built up, go up in flames, it was like I was watching myself disappear in smoke. It felt like I was as evanescent and as insubstantial as was the solid matter of my life in the flames. It felt like I was disappearing along with all that. I remember feeling

'What's left? There's nothing left.' It was just like regular mourning."

At first it seemed a natural reaction to loss, but Alice began to feel haunted by this sense of nothing left, even though she and her husband quickly found another house. Weeks turned into months, and she was still depressed. If she was indeed mourning the loss of her home, it was clearly a severe and abnormal reaction.

Only when she finally went to a therapist did she discover the depth of her mourning: her father had died nearly two years before the house burned down, but she, busy with departmental politics at the college where she taught, had not allowed herself time to mourn properly for him. In fact everyone had admired how well she had "taken it" at the time, and she herself had even been rather proud of it. What happened was that the sense of the frailty of life that came over her the night she stood watching the fire brought back the unfinished mourning for her father, breaking her calm pseudoacceptance of his death.

Mourning cannot achieve its purpose unless you are aware of what or whom you are mourning for. All mourning requires a focus; it needs to be conscious. Once the connection had been made, Alice could see that she still had to mourn for her father and that until she did, she would be "stuck" in inappropriate mourning for the house.

People often deflect their emotions onto a "safe" object as a means of avoiding dealing with the real cause of them. If we refuse to mourn when it is appropriate, we risk finding ourselves in long and deep depression or mourning for a dog or a caged bird. Or we may be caught completely unawares, as was Julie Porter when she complained to me over lunch one day that she had been intensely depressed that past weekend for no reason at all and that the depression still lingered.

It did seem inexplicable at first. Everything was going just fine in her life. She had a prestigious job at high pay which she enjoyed, she was known as the life and soul of any party, and had such a busy social life that she could rarely be found at home. By the time we got to coffee, however, she was talking about an affair that had broken up a year before. It had lasted three years, and she still could not accept that it was over—was still, in fact, plotting ways and means by which she might revive it.

It occurred to me to ask exactly when the breakup had happened. Julie thought a moment, then said, "That's odd. Now you come to mention it, it was exactly a year ago last weekend." She smiled somewhat sheepishly. "Sounds too close for a coincidence, I guess."

It is called "anniversary depression," and catches many of us unawares. Consciously, we manage to repress the memory of what happened a year ago, or even many years ago, on any particular date. But the unconscious remembers. And if there is mourning still to be done, it will surface in the form of depression, insisting on its place in our emotional life.

Lost Love

In many ways, the loss of a loved person to death may be easier to mourn than their loss through separation. Death insists on a physical finality. There can be no lingering hope, conscious or unconscious, that the loss is reversible. But when a marriage or a love affair ends against your will, there is too often the hope against hope that it can be salvaged and re-established, no matter what the odds. This hope works against mourning. Refusing to accept that something is over, we also refuse to mourn. The result is only that we are trapped in the past. Unable to free ourselves of a past love, we cannot find love in the present. Besides, we think, nothing can be as wonderful, as "right," as perfect as that particular relationship. Seen from the perspective of the abandoned lover, every love affair becomes potentially perfect.

"It doesn't make sense," Maria Marshall insisted, banging at the pillows of her sofa. "We were so good together. It's so frustrating. Everything was wonderful, and then suddenly . . ." I reminded her that this had happened a few times already, and though this time it seemed final, the relationship had not been all milk and honey. There had been tears and fights, smaller separations and then ecstatic reunions amidst more tears. It was only a masochist's idea of the ideal relationship. But Maria insisted that it had all the makings of perfection in it. Besides, she added after a while, what was she going to do now?

"We had all our friends in common, we did every-

138

thing together. And now what? Our friends are all couples too. He can find someone else quite easily"— and at this she began to cry again—"but it's different for a woman; it's not that simple. I mean, my whole social life revolved around him. Now what am I going to do?"

Not only had the love been lost, but everything that had been established around it was gone too. Now Maria felt cut off from it all and terribly alone. "Who am I going to go sailing with?" she asked. "I won't be able to go. Who am I going to spend summer weekends with? There won't be anybody; I'll be stuck in town. Does this mean I'm going to start going to singles bars and stuff like that? I can't face it. Honestly, I just can't face it. It feels like my whole life has gone down the drain." She reached for some Kleenex tissues and mopped at her eyes, then looked up suddenly: "You know, it would have been easier if I'd never met him, if he'd never moved in with me, if we'd never spent these two years together. It would have been easier if I'd never loved him at all."

If you have ever had a bad and painful wound, you will know the feeling: the pain is so bad that all you want to do at times is cut out the wound and the sur-rounding flesh so that the pain will stop. Irrational, of course; you know that. But the impulse to tear out or tear off the source of the pain is still there. And we feel the same impulse with psychological pain.

Maria reminded me of Constantine Cavafy's poem "Despair," written when the poet had been abandoned by a lover. Cavafy had "lost him completely, as if he had never been at all." A strong image and a disturbing one—if the lover had never been at all, then a whole section of the poet's life had suddenly been erased from the map of identity. When the lover went, part of Cavafy went too, "lost completely" as though memory were nothing.

Cavafy's means of overcoming his loss was to write both his love and its loss *out* of himself, much like Lady Macbeth washing the imaginary blood from her hands. In effect, he was trying to make himself tabula rasa, to go back to a state of being that preceded both love and loss. And that, of course, is not possible. The past cannot be undone. It remains only to carry it as a burden into the present or to come to terms with it.

The poet had his writing; however much he wanted to negate the past, he knew that by the very act of writing itself, he was working his way through mourning. For Maria, adjusting to her loss would be more difficult. It would involve the whole way she had organized her life. She was now single, no longer coupled, and this radical change in personal status necessitated an equally radical change in the way she lived and thought of her life.

In this situation, many people scramble for other loves, under the illusion that any specific loss can be quickly substituted for. Lose one love and find another quickly, they think, before the mourning catches up with you. They think of their own emotions as some kind of bank vault which must always remain full; when loss occurs, the vaults can be quickly replenished from another source.

It seems to work at first—until the mourning that was never done insinuates itself into the next relationship, breaking it up. Unless there is something wrong with us, we are not machines that can bounce easily from one relationship to the next, as though the only thing lost was the person to be loved. When we lose love, we lose a whole complex of things: contact with that particular person, and the particular warmth and support that they gave us; the world the two people created together; the warmth and security that come simply from *being* loved and from loving in return. Inevitably, we question whether we can still love and whether we are still lovable, but to rush to test out these questions on someone else immediately can only be self-defeating.

Love does not exist in isolation; it is always specific. We don't simply love; we love somebody. And having lost that somebody, that part of ourselves that loved them also feels lost. But it can be found again only within ourselves, not through rushing to someone else. And depression is an essential part of the means of rediscovering it.

For some people, the end of a love affair is especially difficult because there may be no specific ending. The end of a marriage is marked by the ritual of divorce. But for those who are not married, endings may not be so clear.

"I get depressed over endings that never really take place as I want them to," says Art Karloff, a reporter in his midforties who has lived the bachelor life of bars and casual affairs since his divorce ten years ago. "You know, it seems that there should be a proper ending, and very often there isn't. Things just filter off somehow, or are cut off without having reached what I think of as a proper or natural conclusion. I always want to bring things round into a neat circle, and I can't. It's as though if there isn't a proper ending, then whatever it is isn't really finished for me. I can't finish things the way I want, but then I can't leave them unfinished either, and I just end up getting depressed."

True, endings are rarely tidy, but it seems as though Art is using this as his rationale for not coming to terms with them. Unable to work through the ending of one affair, he cannot really bring all of himself to another. Everything remains tentative —"up in the air, somehow," as he put it. He can't commit himself to any deep relationship since he has never quite ended the one before. Avoiding mourning for any specific love, he lives instead in a state of chronic low-grade unresolved depression. He experiences it as boredom, and drinks a lot as though that would kill the sense of his life as a series of unended endings.

Mourning in the form of depression is essential if someone is to love again. Despite our general intolerance of depression, most people do realize that loss of love, whether through death or through separation, does require a period of mourning. But there are many other times too when mourning is both appropriate and important, even though it feels wrong. These are times when the loss is less tangible than love and when we therefore feel guiltier for being depressed. The following chapter takes a look at some of these less tangible forms of the range of loss, all of which resolve, in one way or another, around expectations in conflict with reality.

7 *The Range of Loss*

Poor Catullus, cease your folly
and give up for lost what you see is lost.

*(Miser Catulle, desinas ineptire
Et quod vides perisse perditum ducas)*
Catullus— *Carmina*, viii

The times of depression are very often felt as gaps—
temporary losses of certainty or identity which leave
us feeling empty. There are many such gaps in our
lives: the gap between expectation and reality, for
instance, the gap between self-esteem and the esteem of others, or the gap between how we feel and
how we think we should feel.

One man I know deliberately tries to plan his life,
day by day, so that he will "fill in all the empty
spaces." He admits he is afraid that he would be depressed if he allowed the empty spaces to happen.
But still he occasionally gets depressed. The gaps
slide in without his being able to control them.

Empty spaces are not only a matter of time; they
are psychological spaces too. The awareness of them,
however painful, deepens our appreciation of life's

143

possibilities, and alerts us to our values, our purposes, and the sources of meaning in our lives. Things are never quite as we plan them or as we think they should be, but then life would be very boring indeed if they were.

Great Expectations

Hope is one of the most basic human attributes —an illusion, perhaps, but a life-sustaining one. It gives direction to our lives and creates purpose. But in a consumer society, hope segues easily into expectation.

Take Christmas, New Year's, or Thanksgiving, for example, when a clear image is promoted of how that holiday should be spent and of the happiness it should bring. The media, store promotions, and advertisers all participate in creating this image, and we assent to it, for who, offered the chance of an ideal state of being, would refuse it?

Yet the very explicitness of expectation results too often in disillusion. The single person who has nobody to spend New Year's with or the family person for whom Christmas turns out to be a shambles of family tensions are both haunted by a picture of other people celebrating in perfect warmth, harmony, and happiness.

Indeed, some people, somewhere, might be doing just that. But not everyone, everywhere, and not even most people. We are still victims of the holiday illusion. The conviction lingers that there *is* such a thing as the "perfect" Christmas or New Year's.

And in trying to live up to these images, we face the depression of not achieving them.

Sometimes, a vicious cycle develops as a manic defense swings into play. The more perfection seems unattainable, the more we try to guarantee it, as though if we could just get all the right physical elements into place—people, presents, Yule logs, decorations, turkey—then all the emotional elements would fall into place of themselves.

If we are lucky, we might experience at least one such perfect holiday—and then spend years trying to recapture that perfection, working twice as hard to repeat what is essentially unrepeatable. Perfection and happiness are of the moment, defeating the best of plans. But we still go through the motions in the hope that the motions themselves will generate the right feelings. They never quite do; everything suffers by comparison to the ideal remembered from an earlier time or borrowed from the media. If those comparisons were not available, the feelings we hope for might be more attainable; if we were not so clear in our minds about exactly what we want, we might find it quite easily. But as things are, the joy we are supposed to feel on holidays is so far removed from daily life that we might justifiably wonder what possible cause we could have for depression over not attaining it.

Artificially raised expectations are an emotional plague in a world where the means of raising them are so highly developed. Popular psychology and psychiatry are as guilty in this as the media, encouraging us in the pursuit of an idealized happiness or an impossible personal perfection, and even establishing "norms" for what we "should" have achieved or be doing at any particular stage in our lives. When we are unable to live up to these artificial ideals, we feel let down, as though we had failed ourselves. We have lost the idea of our future selves.

Mike Kaufman, a therapist, has just reached fifty, and looks back with a confused sense of disappointment. "It was especially bad ten years ago, when I was forty," he says, "when it didn't seem like I'd learned anything or like I was any better off in any personal meaningful way."

What does he mean by meaningful? "When I was a little kid," he answers, "it always seemed I would continue to get better and wiser. I never thought in terms of decline. Having less sexual vigor at fifty than at forty bothers me perhaps a little less than average, but I *had* expected to be richer inside, more together, centered. I had expected both to *be* more that way and to be recognized as being more that way. And instead, sometimes I feel neither. I feel as dumb as I was ten years ago, and when I feel dumb, that's very very dumb."

Many of us, comparing ourselves to others, may feel like the character in a *New Yorker* cartoon who complains miserably to his campanion at the bar: "Now I'm too old to be the youngest to do anything anymore." Full of images of what we "should" have done by any certain age, we assess ourselves at such times and find ourselves lacking, our lives proceeding at a more laggardly pace than we had expected or in another direction altogether.

This was brought home to me during an evening with Pat Shaw and Shirley Sommers, both businesswomen in their late forties and both married for the second time. Sophisticated women, they are looked up to by others as practical and wise. But this evening, they felt neither.

"Life has been pretty good, I suppose," said Pat moodily, stirring her coffee even though she took no sugar. "But . . ."

But? She just smiled ruefully. Shirley took up the sentence: "But we never quite imagined that it would be like this. When we were younger, I suppose we always thought that by fifty we'd be comfortable, that we wouldn't have to struggle any more, that life would be easier and we could relax, leave the struggling to younger people."

"But the things we thought we could take for granted, it turns out we can't," Pat continued. "The idea that we'd have reached the peak of our professions and wouldn't have to try so hard any more, or the idea that things would be easier once the children were all out of the house and leading their own lives. . . . We had clear ideas of how life would be, and it's not that way after all. Maybe we just thought that it would all settle down, and we could just stop trying so damn hard." I had never heard Pat swear before. "Instead," she went on, "here I am, nearly fifty, and struggling harder than ever. Oh, it's going well and it's what I want, I know, but it just doesn't seem to be quite natural somehow. . . ."

"It's not the way we expected things to be," Shirley added, nodding in agreement. "It feels as though an established pattern of life has been disrupted, though I'm not even sure how it got established in the first place."

Though neither had set up a rigid code of expectations for themselves, their sense of "shouldness" had been undermined. The mismatch with reality made them feel weary. Expectation had been betrayed by time.

When you are still in your twenties or thirties, it is easy to imagine that though things may not be exactly as you would like them, they may yet turn out that way. The realm of desire still overlaps with the realm of perceived possibility. As time passes, desire remains, but the perception of possibility alters. The whole world is no longer open. Expectations clash with reality, creating a crisis of desire—the crisis of accepting what you have and letting go of the expectation you once had.

The normative ideals of success in the thirties or forties, the fruits of success in the fifties, the beginning of a graceful retirement in the sixties, are far less fluid than we care to admit. Though it is now intellectually commonplace to talk of life as a continual process of development, change, and adaptation, the emotional distance from intellectual comprehension remains vast. Knowing one thing, we still cling to the belief in another.

For instance, there are some who willingly take risks in their lives, justifying the risks in terms both of the payoff if they succeed and the experience if they do not. Yet when the coin of chance turns up tails instead of heads, they suddenly discover that the willingness to risk was not that at all, but a banking on success. Hope had been replaced by expectation, the "maybe" transformed by anticipation into near certainty. As poet Philip Larkin expressed it, "Always too eager for the future, we/Pick up bad habits of expectancy."

While hopes can be dashed and wishes fulfilled or not, expectations involve a far more shattering disillusionment when they do not work out. It is not that we thought we *might* get something; rather, we thought we *were* getting it. We were absolutely certain, as though life were entirely predictable and plannable, and we could run our lives as the rich do their trust funds, with plenty in reserve.

The alternative is to keep everything in reserve, covering yourself against the failure of expectation by restricting your life so that chance cannot turn against you. Hoping to evade depression by evading the possibility of failure, people who do this then find that other kind of depression that focuses on chances *not* taken. Secure but without challenge in their lives, they wonder whether there was any point in it all.

But the issue is not one of challenge and risk; most of us need some form of challenge and search it out. Rather, it is to leave our ideas of the future sufficiently fluid that they can allow for possible differences while still acting as guidelines. The problem lies as much in the way we envision the future as in what we see there.

One can still hope, attempt to fulfill that hope, and, if successful, be pleasantly surprised or gratified. But there is little room for gratification when hope becomes expectation. What happens is, after all, only what we expected.

Postpartum

Sometimes, expectations are so strong that we feel guilty for feeling otherwise. One of the most striking times this happens is in the depression many new parents experience after giving birth.

"It was meant to be the most wonderful experience of my life," said one woman, talking about the birth of her first child. "Instead, it was the most disruptive. It didn't feel wonderful at all. I was depressed for weeks afterward. Everyone was talking about how happy I must be, and I was feeling miserable. I did all the right things, sure. I breastfed her, and I changed her, and I took her out in the pram, but I took no particular pleasure in it. Everything seemed to be in some kind of hiatus. I did know that I didn't want to be this kind of mother, but I didn't know how to be anything else. I didn't know *how* to be a mother. It was like playing a role that nobody ever taught me. I just couldn't get into the part."

Universally, the birth of a child is considered a time for celebration. Most cultures have rituals to mark it—the Jewish *bris,* the Catholic baptism, the secular baby shower—but none of these rituals allow for the common experience of postpartum depression.

"It's meant to be a woman's problem, isn't it?" said one father anxiously, looking back to the birth of his first child some months before. "But do you think there could be such a thing as postpartum depression in men? I mean, there's not meant to be, but if there isn't, then what did I go through?" Another young father, at a loss to explain what happened to him, vainly tried to account for it as "maybe just a sympathetic reaction to my wife's depression." And another concluded that "if it's all a matter of hormones, then the fact that I was depressed must have been a coincidence or something."

There is of course a physical element in postpartum depression, connected to sudden hormonal changes. But the psychological element is just as important, if not more so. Both parents now have a major readjustment to make.

For women, parturition itself is often traumatic; the symbiotic unity of pregnancy is broken in pain. A new separateness has come into being, and the mother must now actively care for the baby instead of simply carrying it within her. In pregnancy, she had perfect control. But after birth, a child exists with needs and a will of its own, yet entirely dependent on its parents for care. Many mothers then feel that what was theirs inside the womb has become an alien existence, and fear that they will never be able to love their own child.

When this happens, guilt aggravates the depression. Expecting joy and finding none, the new mother blames herself, wondering if she is "unnatural." Yet this happens to so many women—up to two thirds in one estimate—that analyst Therese Benedek could even write that "fortunate is the mother whose love for the child wells up as she hears the first cry." If this is fortunate, then the norm is something else—a period of adjustment in which the mother has to adapt to *being* a mother. This new role is a significant and unalterable break in the way she sees herself and in the way her husband sees her.

Both mother and father have lost a previous state of existence. Where there were two, there are now three. The wife has to adjust to her husband seeing her not only as a lover but also as the mother of his child. The father has to make the same adjustment. From being a couple, they have become a family.

She may fear that her new role as mother will make her less sexually attractive to her husband; he may fear that the child will displace him in his wife's affection. Moreover, the birth of the child may increase his felt burden of responsibility. At a time when many people do not get married until they decide they want a child, the birth becomes a psychological stamp of seriousness. From being a young man, the husband has become a family man.

Both parents are thus anxious about how they will fulfill their new responsibilities and still retain the bond they had before the birth. Moreover, they must both now readjust their perceptions of themselves on the generational scale. Where previously they were daughter and son, they now face the sometimes perplexing situation of being both mother and daughter, father and son.

In this new abundance of roles, their time perception also changes. A child may not think beyond the immediate present, an adolescent beyond the evening, or a college student beyond the next batch of exams. But new parents must think in terms of two decades of responsibility. Envisioning the child as an adult, they glimpse their own middle age and are frightened by it. Their lives are no longer quite their own, but have been predetermined to some extent by the birth of their child. Depression at such times can be an essential period of withdrawal in order to absorb the prospect of a new, long-term future.

This becomes even clearer when we look at other forms of postpartum depression. It is a well-known phenomenon among writers, for instance, who may spend a year or two or even far more working on one book. One would think that when they finish it, they would be elated and relieved. They themselves expect that. And yet when the time comes, there is suddenly the terrible empty feeling of "What do I do now? Where do I go from here? There's nothing left to write, nothing left at all."

Something that had defined their lives for a considerable period of time is suddenly gone, finished, and sent out into the world of publishing to sink or swim on its own terms. They have lost control over it. It is, in a sense, no longer theirs. In this respect, writers experience something very close to the postpartum depression of birthing women. The common metaphor of "giving birth" to a book may be more apt than anyone had imagined.

Building a house, doing a research report, finishing a set of final exams—all these types of experience can be the preludes to postpartum depression, even though it seems self-evident that they should be the occasion for happiness. In all of them, that gap appears. Challenge is gone, purpose is gone, and the people involved now have to create new challenge and purpose. Their lives now require a certain redefinition. For a while, they are no longer quite sure who they are, or why.

A Streetcar Named Success

The gap between how we feel and how we expect to feel at any certain time confounds ideals and wishes. If we achieve an ideal or fulfill a wish, what then? What do we wish for in the future? Though it seems an irony, it makes perfect sense that one of the times when it seems that there is nothing left to wish for—and when we therefore feel depressed—is when a wish has been fulfilled. Often, this is the time of success.

In 1947, Tennessee Williams published an essay in the *New York Times* about his sudden success three years before. Until that time, he wrote, his life "had required endurance, a life of clawing and scratching." But when *The Glass Menagerie* became a hit, the playwright needed to claw no longer:

"I was unaware of how much vital energy had gone into this struggle until the struggle was removed. I was out on a level plateau with my arms still thrashing and my lungs still grabbing at air that no longer resisted. This was security at last. I sat down and looked about me and was suddenly depressed." For three months, "I was walking around dead in my shoes, and I knew it but there was no one I knew or trusted sufficiently, at that time, to take him aside and tell him what was the matter."

For years, someone may have aimed for a particular goal; the attainment of this goal becomes the pinnacle of happiness in their scheme of things. Then, by dint of hard work and probably good fortune too, they reach it. But exactly at this point, when they and anyone else would expect them to be the happiest they have ever been, something else suddenly happens. Much to their confusion, they feel emptied and purposeless, as though a gap had opened up in their lives. And so it has: their wish is gone. It has been gratified, and therefore no longer exists as wish but as reality. What then is there left to wish for? And how does one exist without wishing, without projecting oneself forward into the future with a purpose?

The higher the experience, often the harder the fall. Astronaut Buzz Aldrin was one of the first men to walk on the moon—not only his own dream, but the dream of generations of human beings. In his case, he had literally to come back to earth, and there, for months, he suffered deep depression. He had fulfilled a dream and now had to face the long hard struggle of reconciling himself to life on earth with its inevitable shortcomings, to the commercialization and even trivialization of his experience, and to the fact that for him, there was no longer any ultimate challenge. What do you do after you've been to the moon? For a long time, there was no answer to the question "What now?"

Aldrin's experience was of course practically unique, but on a lesser level, those people lucky enough to succeed face basically the same dilemma. They have translated the future into the present—and suddenly, though the present may seem full, the future is empty. They no longer know what to wish for.

This happened to Phil Berner, who realized his major life's wish in his early forties, when he got the top producer's job he had always aimed for in television. It was one of the most enviable jobs in the whole business. Yet within a few weeks of moving to his new post, Phil was depressed.

He complained of how slow it seemed compared to the hectic pace of his previous post on the evening news. He missed the constant ferment and excitement of things happening "now, now, now." "It's too soft," he kept saying of the new job. "Somehow it was more exciting from the outside, when I wanted to do it. Now that I'm actually doing it, the gleam's gone out of it. It's not a challenge any more."

He began to play with the idea of moving back to his former post in "hard news," refusing to consider that even if he did so, the basic problem would still remain: the challenge had gone out of his life. The specific goal he had aimed for was now his, and he had no new one. The desire to go back was partly the illusion that he could drown that fact in hectic activity, but there was also a kind of magical thinking involved: part of the old job had been the aiming for the new one; if he returned to it, he might recover that aim.

We all long to be at the top or on easy street, but those who reach it often feel defeated by their own success. Their life seems to be missing a vital element, one they find hard to pinpoint since by definition, life at the top should have it all. Even to admit that something is missing is to give the lie to everything they have always believed. But the truth is that when they no longer have to struggle, the struggle itself is missing.

"Success happened to me," wrote Tennessee Williams. "But once you fully apprehend the vacuity of a life without struggle you are equipped with the basic means of salvation." For him, depression was the means of gaining that understanding; it was the means to re-gaining desire and the need to write again.

But Phil Berner had to find his way through depression more slowly. After sounding out various people in the network, he realized that he would not be permitted to go backward in the organization. Playwrights may walk away from success, but not television producers. Phil had to come to terms with his new job gradually, and he did it by seeking out more and more difficult topics to deal with—the kinds of issues that nobody else wanted to cover because they were too complex or too elusive, or because they had no glamour. At first it was an unconscious search; then gradually it became conscious as he realized what he was doing.

It was hard; each time, he dealt with subjects in which he had little or no previous experience, and had to start from scratch. But this was challenging. In the lack of a major challenge, he found that he could create a constant flow of smaller ones, and these in turn added up to a very different goal in life—not in terms of his own job or income or status, but in terms of the quality of what he was doing and of the program as a whole. It took a year, but out of depression, he created a new and satisfying sense of purpose.

In High Esteem

We need to feel that we are worthwhile and that what we do is worthwhile. Psychologically, this is known as self-esteem—an idea which rose rapidly through the ranks of psychological theory in the seventies. Clearly it is important, and directly addresses the issue of what we value and why, of what our values are. But as the acknowledged stock of self-esteem has risen, many people have begun to confuse values with aims.

Aims such as success have become values in and of themselves. Self-esteem therefore rises and falls with the degree of success, while success itself is generally defined in external terms—by what others see and envy. Thus self-esteem is in danger of becoming merely a mirror of the esteem of others. The idea that one might be successful without outside acknowledgment seems to be almost a contradiction in terms.

This was much in my mind when I saw Peter Schaffer's play *Amadeus,* which focused on the rivalry between Mozart and court composer Salieri. Mozart, though egoistically rampant with self-esteem, failed to find acceptance for the music now regarded as one of the pinnacles of Western culture, and died a pauper. Salieri was held in great respect in his day, even though he is now remembered almost solely for his connection with Mozart. The conflict that interested Schaffer was not Mozart's but Salieri's: despite the abundant esteem of others, Salieri knew how mediocre his own work was compared to Mozart's, and suffered through guilt, envy, and self-hate as he succeeded almost despite himself while Mozart's brilliance went virtually ignored.

After seeing the play, I could not help wondering how many in the audience would not prefer to be Salieri—talented but not superbly so, yet highly esteemed in his own time. Salieri, it seemed to me, was the modern man, his sensibility and his situation far closer to our own than that of Mozart but with one major difference: despite his success, he could not see himself as successful. His system of values ran so deep that he could not allow himself to internalize the esteem of others without good cause, and the very fact of Mozart's existence had taken away the cause.

Today, the system for reflecting the esteem of others is far more developed. In the age of the mass media, the quality of others' esteem and the reasons for it are less important than the very fact of its existence. Notoriety equals fame; noise is more important than content. We now respect the trappings of success—the attention, the money—to the degree that if one has fulfilled a lifetime ambition or simply done a good job, one has not "really" succeeded unless one is publicly recognized as having done so. This has had a pernicious effect on self-esteem; though essentially a private quality, it has gone public.

Public esteem is a fickle business. In the fifties, women who devoted their lives to raising a family and running the lives of their husbands and children were highly approved socially; today, someone is liable to say "Yes, but what do you *do*?" as though they did nothing but lie on a chaise longue all day waiting for the family to come home. In the Second World War, homecoming soldiers were greeted with fanfare and admiration; after the Vietnam War, they were quietly ignored. I have seen brilliant writers question their own abilities because their books do not sell widely on the commercial market, and topflight laywers and doctors abandon public service for the more lucrative and highly esteemed fields of private practice.

All these people faced the same basic dilemma: to do what they believed was right and should therefore boost their self-esteem, despite the fact that it gained no esteem from others and therefore lowered their self-esteem. One person who has struggled with this dilemma throughout his career is Len Murphy, a police officer in a particularly crime-troubled East Coast city. Len has survived riots and gun-fights, tire-burning car chases and intra-station politics, and soon he'll be up for retirement. He's more than ready for it.

"You see a lot of depression among police officers," he says. "It's not like with other men who hardly talk to each other. You get out there in the car with your buddy, you're in the radio car together for eight hours at a stretch, and you're closer to him than you are to your wife. So you know how the guys feel. And right now it's especially tough. Guys can't wait to get out. They get no backing from the courts, no backing from the public any more. The respect is gone. You know, when I first joined the force, I was 'Mister.' Now I'm a pig. Now a cop is a target."

In retrospect, he wouldn't do it over again. "Maybe

I would in some small town somewhere down south, but not here, not in this place, no way. It's like everything worthwhile's been taken out of the job. It's not the pay—we have enough for our needs, and we don't strive for the moon. It's not that. It's just that, you know, you want some respect for the job you're doing. It's a good job; it's an important job. But people never realize those things until they get into some kind of trouble and need a cop."

The public lack of faith and respect has affected his own, and "Sure, I get depressed. You know, the feeling of 'Ah the hell with it, is it worth it?' But it passes. It never lasts long with me. You know, one guy says, 'Laugh it off.' Another says, 'Get a punching bag, punch it out.' Me, what do I do? I yell. At the boss or whoever, I let it out. And I don't mean wasting powder either."

All in all, he's simply relieved to have come through in one piece. "I've never been fed up with life," he says, "though I may have been fed up often with the *way* I live. It's funny, you know, but till you get off the boat and look back and see what the ocean looks like, you don't realize what a rough ride you've had. I wouldn't join a metropolitan force today. I think I've been a good cop, done a good job, raised a good family. I have no regrets about the way I've lived. I just wouldn't do it again, that's all."

Like Len Murphy, we all need a sense of significance and are vulnerable to depression when it is threatened. We need to feel not only that we have a place in the world, but that this place is acknowledged by others. When this acknowledgment is lacking, depression becomes a crisis of self-esteem.

Self-esteem depends on faith in the significance of what you are doing. It depends on the meaning you make out of your life. But your vocabulary of meaning needs to be understood, used, and appreciated by those around you too. It is hard to cling to it in isolation.

One man, now in his forties, remembers the bitter letdown of doing something he knew was good as a child and of receiving no recognition for it. "I was thirteen, and my brother, who's a year older than I, was kept back a year at school. Since we couldn't be in the same class because we were brothers, he was put into a parallel class. The kids there were very tough, and he was miserable. So I offered to swap with him. It felt like I was going into the lions' den, but I managed it. I managed so well, in fact, that these really tough kids voted me head of the homeroom. And I remember coming home and telling my mother about it—and she just cut me down for it, like what was so great about it all? And that experience of achieving something and then finding out that it makes no impression on the person you most want to impress—that makes public recognition very important afterward."

Yet like this man, however insignificant we may feel when depressed, we are also convinced, deep down, that we should not *have* to feel this way. We do not doubt our own ability so much as suffer because others do not recognize it.

I suspect that our sense of self-esteem is far less vulnerable than most theorists would have us believe. Others may see us as insignificant, but we are not really convinced that we are so, and we struggle against internalizing society's view of us. Although a major psychoanalytic theory of depression sees it as "anger turned inward," expressed in an inordinate amount of self-blame and self-accusation, this does not seem to apply so strongly to normal depression. We blame the world rather than ourselves.

This, I think, accounts for much of the feeling of "not fair"—we feel that we *do* deserve better and *are* better than the world gives us credit for. We refuse to accept the world's view of us, and see the loss of others' esteem as an attack on our values.

In response, some may compromise their values (which itself can be intensely depressing until they manage to forget what their original values were). Others may choose the "cognitive therapy" route, changing their perceptions of how the world sees them and thus eventually, while avoiding depression, living in a world almost entirely of their own making. Still others may finally succumb to the view of others, internalizing their lack of esteem to lack of self-esteem. But I believe that most of us do none of these. Like Len Murphy, we struggle on through. And if the price of that struggle is depression, it is still worth it.

Perhaps after all, Salieri and Mozart were simply on opposite sides of the same situation. Both suffered a gap between self-esteem and the esteem of others. But while Mozart, at least in Peter Schaffer's version of things, hardly even noticed that gap for most of his life, Salieri was painfully aware of it. Of the two, he was perhaps the better man—the man of values, and therefore the one to question the esteem of others, even though he had it, and to be depressed.

Retired From the Game

Much of our self-esteem comes from the work we do. In fact, when we meet someone new who wants to know who we are, we introduce ourselves almost automatically as "a doctor" (or a journalist or a manager or whatever it is we do). We present ourselves to the world through our work.

What happens, then, when we no longer work? Those who have been fired and cannot find new employment suffer a drastic fall in self-esteem. But often so do those who retire, even though they may have been looking forward to it for years.

It would be hard to go through retirement without experiencing some degree of depression. A smooth adjustment is virtually impossible, for the rules of one's life have changed and changed drastically. The name of the game is completely different. One is no longer quite sure how to present oneself to the world; "being retired" seems not quite enough. In one's work role, one felt significant. Now, a nagging feeling of insignificance surfaces; one feels isolated from the mainstream, out of the main game of life.

"It is a matter of everyday observation that men suffer grievously when they can find no games worth playing," wrote Thomas Szasz. The games he was talking about were nothing playful; they were the serious games of life which create a sense of significance. And in retirement, "the game worth playing" —work—has been lost. For many new retirees, this is experienced as a feeling of reduced being.

Joseph Pelliter took early retirement from his medical practice because of a bad heart condition. He could have become a part-time consultant, but his doctor advised against it. His pension would allow him and his wife to live quite comfortably, together with what he had accumulated over the years from playing the market a little. But the problem was what to do with the retirement he had been saving up for over the past thirty-five years. As his wife nervously pointed out, "You can't spend the rest of your life playing golf and bridge." '

The first few weeks went smoothly enough. While his wife continued her volunteer and social activities, Joseph stayed home and to his surprise took great pleasure in not having to work. He read, worked a little in the garden, took an afternoon nap, and played both golf and bridge. The phone was quiet, but that seemed a relief. The children visited, made sure that everything was all right, and went off again. Then the depression came.

It lasted several weeks, and took him completely by surprise. "It all seemed very appealing at first," he said, "the quiet life and all that. But then one morning there just seemed no point in getting out of bed. I didn't know what to do with myself if I did get up. There seemed no reason to do anything. I felt lost, like I'd been ejected from the world. *Re*jected, I suppose is more like it. Finally I walked into the bathroom and began to shave, wondering why on earth I was even bothering to do this, and found myself thinking about getting an open razor so that I could let it slip and quietly cut my throat. And then I just stared at myself in the mirror in horror that I'd thought such a thing. . . .

"You see, all this gardening, chess, bridge, and so on, it was all fine so long as I was relaxing from work. But I wasn't relaxing from work any longer. I didn't know what to do with myself. I just felt completely lost."

Throughout Joseph's life, work had been one thing and play quite another. Work was the serious business, and the rest was more of a dessert to the main course. Now there was suddenly no answer to the question "What do you do?"—or none, that is, in terms of employment. And in the lack of an answer, he felt unable to do anything at all.

When the phrase "a productive member of society" is practically synonymous with "good citizen," this crisis is all the more severe. The retiree has to establish his or her own personal sense of "doing" as opposed to the commonly accepted one, which is considered almost exclusively in terms of remunerative employment. But this takes time. It demands a reassessment which can often take place only in depression. As Joseph Pelliter put it, "You feel you don't quite belong in the world anymore." You feel less a person, less solid, less rooted. A major means of defining yourself vis-à-vis the world is gone. That loss has to be mourned, and out of that mourning, new meaning constructed.

"There's still the respect accorded a retired doctor, of course," said Joseph, "but now the problem is what do I respect myself for? For what I've done in the past, or for what I'm doing right now? I don't want to live entirely on the past. So I'll have to find something that can really involve me now, something interesting in itself." When we talked, he was considering a few ideas: enrolling in a course on political science, volunteering his services to the local branch of his political party, buying a computer and learning a whole new language. . . . The future and its possibilities had begun to open up for him. "I had no idea how limited my world was outside of work," he said. "But now's my chance to change that." There were games worth playing other than work, he began to discover, and games that might also be fun.

The Empty Nest

Role changes determined by age are particularly difficult to handle. We are never quite ready to be as old as we are. The answer to "Who am I?" might be objectively changed, but we have not yet made the psychological adaptation.

The mother of a newborn child may want to be mothered herself. A middle-aged man feels threatened as he sees younger men advancing past him in his field. Stories of whiz kids make us all feel "My God, but I'm ten years older than that and what have I done?" But one of the hardest role changes may be when a mother is no longer needed as a mother—when the children have left home or are no longer as dependent on her as before.

It is known somewhat cutely as "the empty nest syndrome," though birds do not appear to suffer from it. And it refers to what happens when children leave the "nest" that the mother has spent years creating and caring for.

Despite the influence of feminism, half of American wives still do not work outside their homes. And although feminist theorists may define the housewife as everything from fashion designer to accountant to chef, many housewives feel an erosion of self-respect, as though they belonged to a group that has survived past its viable time. Waking up to the fact that there is not that much satisfaction in simply keeping house, many focus their means of fulfillment on their children, as though the children's accomplishments at baseball or school could become theirs. They live to a large extent for and through the children.

Ellen Seamans, for instance, was always a woman of relentless good spirits. She smiled and kept a good face on things no matter what, and looked so young that she was often admired for seeming to be the sister of her own children rather than the mother. But then came the time when her teenage daughters were no longer dependent on her; they began moving away from her and into their own independent lives. Slowly, Ellen began to suffer from a discomforting awareness that she had given up much in her own life for a role that would soon no longer be needed at all. For the first time since she herself was a teenager, she allowed herself to become depressed.

"I just didn't know what there was for me to do," she said later. "For the first time in my life I felt I was really getting old, that life was passing me by. It seemed ridiculous to even think of starting over at forty. I mean, I always wanted to be a painter and kept it up a little over the years, but to start taking it seriously so late in life seemed silly. What I'd taken seriously was the family, and now suddenly I felt they weren't taking *me* seriously, that there was nothing left for me to do. Cheering Martin up at the end of a hard day's work and giving nice dinner parties wasn't enough. There had to be more."

In that realization, gained through depression, Ellen avoided the solution of many full-time house-wives—an almost fanatic insistence on absolute cleanliness and tidiness. Many women are con-stantly polishing and dusting what they have pol-ished and dusted only the day before; in so doing, they may be searching for perfection in at least one attainable area of their lives. If the myth of the per-fect marriage propagated by Hollywood, romance novels, and advertising is unrealistic, then at least the image of the perfect home can still be main-tained.

Yet when utopia is defined as nothing more than a shining floor, every housewife is aware, at some level, of a sense of loss—loss of real productive satis-faction, of struggle and of meaning. The meaning of a perfectly shiny floor is too often that there *is* no other meaning.

Those who dub this loss of meaning "housewife's depression" avoid the real issue, treating it as though it were a separate diagnostic category myste-riously connected with the fact of being a housewife, with its own specific pattern of symptoms. Yet it is quite easy to understand within the framework of normal depression. To be depressed in such a situa-tion makes sense; the problem remains that for fear of facing the depression, many women never really emerge from it. They fill the nest with busy work.

But the empty nest syndrome is not confined to full-time housewives. Even those who least expect it often experience it. Julia Wexler, for instance, is a special-education counselor in the Midwest, whose life appeared an ideal balance between work and family—a full life in which there seemed to be no room for emptiness.

Then the family dog died. It was a mutt, with as much gray hair by then as black, a bad limp from the three traffic accidents it had survived, and a somewhat battered look from having lived thirteen years with three boisterous youngsters. It was a fixture in the household, taken for granted. It died in its sleep. And Julia went into a deep depression.

She knew that she was mourning the dog and knew too that the depth of her mourning was exaggerated. But she couldn't help it. "I miss him much more than I thought I would," she said. "He was part of the whole family, of the kids being born and growing up. And now that he's gone, it seems that everything's gone. The kids are nearly grown, they're out of the house most of the time, and I feel like I've become just a provider of meals and clean linens in some temporary way station in their lives that they conveniently call home. Soon they'll start to leave home altogether, one by one. It's the end of a whole era."

But the dog's dying had not been the only death in the family. Over a year before, Julia's mother had been killed in a traffic accident. She lived in another city, and somehow Julia felt guilty, as though if she had been there, the accident would not have happened. Though she mourned her mother, guilt about not having been a good enough daughter was mixed in with the grief. Back home, she had put all that aside as best she could—until the dog's death.

Though it seems clear enough to an outsider, the connection between her mother's death and the dog's death had to be pointed out to her—and the further connection between the loss of her mother and the impending loss of her own mothering role.

Parents are never quite ready for their children to lead autonomous lives. It undermines the important role of being a parent in their own lives, and underscores the fact that they too are now older. As children leave home, parents see their own old age advancing on them. And although this has generally been seen as specifically a woman's problem, since the role of mother has been taken more seriously by most theorists and therapists than that of father, men too suffer from it.

Gregory Morrison thought that he'd come through it all rather well. It had been difficult seeing the children leave, true, but he had managed quite well, he thought. Now that he was in his midfifties, he was generally pleased with life. The children seemed to be happily married, his work as a management consultant was going well, and he and his wife could look forward to a comfortable future.

One Sunday, he took an afternoon walk through the park. His wife had stayed at home that afternoon, preferring to read, but the sunshine and the feeling of spring in the air had enticed him out. It was a fine time just to relax and take in what was happening.

The park was full of people. Children ran and played Frisbees, flew kites and chased after balls, or called to their parents to watch as they did a somersault on the grass. They tugged at adults' hands, pleading for an ice-cream cone, or just walked hand in hand with their parents, secure in the feeling of protection while gazing at everything happening on the grass. All around him, Gregory heard childish voices: "Dad, hey, Dad, look!" "Daddy, can I have some cotton candy?" "Dad, can we go to the pond?" And suddenly he felt a terrible sense of emptiness, of something very missing.

"It was so strong I felt it physically, in my chest, on the left side where the heart is. A real sharp pain, as I just stood there and longed for a child beside me, hand in mine, longed for the voice of a young child of my own saying, Daddy, Daddy, let's do things. And I just stood still and looked at all these young men with their young children, and tears came to my eyes because I had none any more and never would again."

He walked slowly home, the pain still there. When he reached the house, he paused a while before entering, trying to talk himself out of it. "Gregory," he said to himself, "you're fifty-four now, you're not twenty-eight any longer. You had that, you had the children, and now it's over, that's gone now. Now it's a different time of your life."

The pain abated as he talked to himself, but not entirely. The memory of it stayed with him physically for the rest of the day. And for some days after, he felt a heavy sadness until that too passed.

"It's so strange," he said. "I'm pleased with the present, life is good. And yet the past just catches you at times like that, and you realize all that you've lost. The present becomes irrelevant, and all you want is to have the past again. Of course you can't, and you know that, but what you know doesn't always determine what you feel. It was such a beautiful day, and I felt so relaxed—perhaps the past just slipped in on me." And he smiled, shrugged, and returned a little sadder to the present.

8 *The Thought of Suicide*

> Darkling I listen; and, for many a time
> I have been half in love with easeful death.
>
> JOHN KEATS, *Ode to a Nightingale*

Suzanne Maitlin is a senior marketing executive; like many others in the hectic top levels of her profession, she lives for her work and relaxes by talking shop. She was doing that when we met at a mutual friend's house, so I was surprised when, hearing that I was researching depression, she drew me away from the others to the far corner of the living room. There, she ignored the professional talk going on around the coffee table and told me instead about what had happened to her the day before.

It had been a hard day. She had been taking antibiotics for an infection and they were draining her of energy, yet she had to go to an important business meeting. "It was vital I be there," she said. The meeting involved drinking. It went poorly, and after it she went home and had another couple of drinks.

Mixing liquors and antibiotics is never the best of ideas, so it was predictable that she would have a bad evening. But she was unprepared for just how bad it would be. The frustration and disappointment of the afternoon mixed with the antibiotics and alcohol to wear down her resistance, and she fell into an acute depression. For hours, she sat thinking what she called "strange thoughts, terrible thoughts."

She thought about taking every sleeping pill and tranquilizer in her bathroom cabinet and washing them down with whatever alcohol was left in the apartment. Instead, in the end she simply fell asleep, waking up the next morning with a terrible hangover . . . and the memory of the night before.

Those thoughts had obviously shaken her. They shake most of us. If we find ourselves contemplating suicide, even for a moment, we are both terrified and horrified—as much, it seems, by the very fact that we are thinking of it as by the idea itself.

It may be just the thought of letting the razor slip, or an idea that comes to mind as you look down from the top of a tall building. Stand on the top of the World Trade Center in Manhattan, and the fences to prevent suicides may make you think of the possibility of your own; stand on San Francisco's Golden Gate Bridge, and the thought of all the known suicides off that bridge may make you wonder if you could join that number. Or it may be the more serious calculation of how many sleeping pills or what height of window would be necessary to ensure "success." Yet though it seems that the idea has occurred to at least half of us at one time or another, and quite possibly to far more of us than that, the thought of suicide remains the least talked about element of depression and the most shameful. And because suicide fantasies are so rarely mentioned, we are all the less prepared for them when they occur.

Suicide, after all, is seen as the ultimate mental sickness, literally fatal. We pity those who have killed themselves, and yet fear them too, even though they are dead; we fear the awareness of that total despair that we know must have driven them to the act. We would rather not know that such despair is possible. And if it is, we label it sickness. As Suzanne Maitlin said that evening, "I had no idea that I was even capable of thinking such thoughts. Where did they come from? What does it mean? Am I really sick?"

Confronting the Possibility

If we think about suicide, we feel that we have entered a dark and utterly irrational realm of emotion, as though we are suddenly cut adrift from the main current of humanity so devoted to life. We feel beyond the pale. If suicide itself is beyond the bounds of socially determined acceptability, then so too must be the thought of it. We feel as though by just thinking about it, we had somehow taken part in the act itself.

But fantasizing one's own death does not make one an actual suicide, any more than wishing somebody dead in a fit of temper or acute disappointment makes one a murderer, or daydreaming about robbing a bank makes one a criminal. For the vast majority of people, such ideas are not guidelines to action so much as an imaginative playing with an ever-present possibility. We flirt with the idea of suicide simply because it *is* possible. What Freud called "the game of life" is also the game of death. By playing it, we explore; by using imagination, we experience the possibility of causing our own deaths without actually endangering our lives.

Some may do this in a more indirect way—by imagining their own funerals, for instance, with the actual manner of death left conveniently vague. "When I was younger," remembers a woman in her forties, "I would dream about my own funeral. Everyone would say how sad it was, my dying so young and with my potential and so on, and everyone would be crying and crying. And I was there too, and they'd be talking to me and they'd come up and shake my hand, and say things like 'Your hand is so cold,' and then I'd realize that I didn't feel anything, and *then* I realized that I was the body. . . ."

Such dreams played out on an unconscious level the sense of inner death she felt in her waking life when she was depressed. Many others play this out in daydreams, rerunning the details of the funeral through their minds until it becomes satisfyingly supportive since everyone talks about how much they loved and will miss you. When you emerge from such a daydream, the real world seems very empty and gray for a while as you come to terms with the fact that you are still alive. You have died a little in fantasy; now it is time to get on with the harder business of living.

This kind of playing with the idea of one's own

death is no mere pastime or childish game, nor the kind of game that people refer to nowadays when they tell someone to "stop playing games." It is a genre of another order: by playing with the idea of our own deaths, we are also playing with the meaning of our life—exploring it, searching for it. The possibility of ending our own lives is inevitably a challenge to the way we live them.

Philosophers have long appreciated this seeming paradox. Schopenhauer called death "the muse of philosophy." Nietzsche claimed that the thought of suicide has saved many lives. Gabriel Marcel maintained that "the fact that suicide is always possible is the essential starting point of any genuine metaphysical thought"—any thought, that is, that concerns the whole question of our existence, of the terms by which we exist, and of how we do or would wish to exist.

These are among the most uncomfortable questions that can be asked. Thinking about being always involves thinking about *not* being too, just as thinking about depression also involves thinking about happiness. This is why we try to evade such thinking, attempting not to think *about* existence, but simply to exist. We might allow ourselves to think about the "tactics" by which we live, but still we shy away from thinking about life itself—until suicide fantasies catch us up short. Suddenly, we are aware of the fact of our own existence.

For Martin Heidegger, this idea affords the first glimpse of a possible "authentic existence." Once truly grasped as possibility, he maintained, death is present in human existence from birth; confronting death as possbile, we are torn out of the context of a banal life and restored to a self which must face mortality without disguise. Heidegger called this confrontation "freedom-towards-death." As he saw it, the perpetual possibility of nothingness—of the non-existence of self—rests on the awareness of this very existence. In the confrontation with death, then, we emerge feeling more alive.

Raising the Ante

The life of danger heightens the awareness of the possibility of death—and therefore the vitality of life. "Life is impoverished, it loses in interest," wrote Freud, "when the highest stake in the game, life itself, may not be risked."

While most of us can conceive of nonbeing in the imagination, some are driven to risk their lives in fact. Sometimes it even seems that they have a death wish or are trying to commit suicide in a socially approved way. The mountaineer, the racing driver, the test pilot—even flamboyantly "successful" suicides such as Ernest Hemingway or Sylvia Plath—are, in a sense, acting out for the rest of us. The closer their brushes with death, the more the rest of us are absolved from brushing against it too closely ourselves. They give us heroics instead of the fear and trembling with which we think of suicide. And therefore we idealize them.

We romanticize those who have been on the brink of death—who have "smelled" it, in the term used by popular writers, and survived to tell what it smells like. It seems to be a heady smell, intoxicating and seductive. We can sense it in dangerous sports; we can even participate in it through fiction or theater. Through our heroes of danger, we can live vicariously on the brink or on the wire. Through their extremes, they absolve us from thinking about the possibility of causing our own deaths.

When the taboo against killing is lifted, as in wartime, this romanticization can reach an extreme. The awareness of the possibility of death seems to give the sense of being alive a particular sharpness and poignancy. In *Thoughts for the Times on War and Death,* written at the start of World War I, Freud saw it as "evident that war is bound to sweep away the conventional treatment of death. Death will no longer be denied; we are forced to believe in it. People really die; and no longer one by one, but many, often tens of thousands, in a single day. . . . Life has, indeed, become interesting again; it has recovered its full content."

Those who have not fought in a war have a certain admiring awe of those who have, as though since they have "known" death through fighting—through being in contact with it and even causing it—they had gained some other kind of knowledge as well, like Greek heroes returning from the underworld. Sometimes this awe may be well placed. Those who have killed in war and yet retained a sense of themselves—by which I mean a full sense of the horror of what they have done and of the thin balance between life and death, and a consequently increased respect for the fragility and value of life—are indeed in a certain sense set apart. They have a knowledge that most of us prefer to step back from. It is this knowledge that we begin to approach in suicide fantasies, and find terrifying. (It should be added, however, that not all those who kill in war come through it with this respect for life; in fact it may be that only a minority do so. Some are coarsened by it; a few even boast of their killing, and this in itself is a means of denying the knowledge they saw but rejected in horror—the knowledge of the fragility of their own lives.)

But despite the terror, the truth is also that suicide fantasies are exciting, just as heroes' adventures and war are exciting. By bringing us close to death, even if only in the imagination, they raise the ante. Thinking of suicide may at first seem an extreme means to do this, but is it really more extreme than driving too fast or taking risks when mountaineering? Rather, it seems, the one is a conscious flirtation with suicide, the other an unconscious one (not so far removed, perhaps, from the dangerous driving or self-destructive drinking that often typify masked depression). When everything seems dull and devoid of excitement, as it does in depression, the thought of suicide itself has the excitement of drama, of action, and of the forbidden.

Carl Tanner, an engineer, looks back on a time of acute depression and on the suicide fantasies he entertained with a strange kind of fondness. He was steeling himself for a divorce and haunted by the feeling of having failed as a husband. Now he sounds almost wistful. "It was so *strong*," he says, with a touch of awe. "The intensity of it was amazing. I never knew I could feel that strongly." He thought about the river, about a gun, about a razor; thought about all the people who had killed themselves before him, "especially in the Depression, I could really understand all those bankers jumping out of windows"; thought about the arrangements he should make for his family before doing anything. In retrospect, he says, that depression was the strongest he had ever felt about anything. He had never experienced his own aliveness as strongly as when he envisaged ending it. Anguishing though it was, he still cannot help looking back with a certain longing for the high emotional coloration his life took on in those weeks. When he placed himself on the brink, he felt as though he were at the core of life.

The connection between sexuality and death—as dark and terrifying to most of us as the thought of suicide and just as little mentioned—underlines the way life and death play off against each other. Sexuality is associated with vitality—indeed, with the source of life itself—and is therefore the antithesis of death. It is hardly surprising, then, that depression generally involves a loss of sexual interest (except when it is masked or denied, when sexual promiscuity becomes a means of fending off self-awareness). But when the ante is raised to death itself, it should also not be surprising that close contact with death or a narrow escape from it can be accompanied by intense sexuality.

A friend who was with the first American forces liberating the Nazi concentration camps in 1945, for instance, vividly remembers the rush of male and female survivors toward each other. With a mixture of awe and respect, he relates the sight of living skeletons copulating openly and publicly. It seemed to him to be an immediate and automatic reaction of "I'm alive"—a reassertion of life in the midst of death. In that place, what would be incomprehensible under normal circumstances was a painful and shocking yet superbly human response to death and annihilation, an atavistic defiance that arouses both revulsion and admiration.

Another friend, a New Yorker, clearly remembers the night she and her husband saw a young man shot in the street during a robbery. By the time the ambulance arrived, he was dead. Shaken, the two went home; after a large glass of cognac each, they went to bed. And there, to her shamed amazement, they made love quickly and urgently and only then fell asleep, exhausted.

"In retrospect, it seems such a terrible thing to do after what had happened in the street," she said. "It seemed terrible at the time too, but it was automatic somehow. Like we were fighting off death. We never talked about it between us, but I'm sure that's what it was."

These stories come from the encounter with actual death. In both instances, sexuality was an acting out of vitality in the shadow of death. But in metaphorical death—the inner death or little death of depression, where something within has been lost—the acting out takes place in the imagination.

When we imagine taking our own lives, we create a physical symbol for the inner death we feel. And since we are symbolic creatures, if we can acknowledge that symbol and discover what it stands for, we do not need to act it out in reality. This is what Nietzsche meant when he remarked that the thought of suicide had saved many lives. Suicide fantasies are not the random thoughts of a despairing or a sick mind; they are an imaginative acting out of how we feel. Fantasies of our own funerals have the same purpose: we mourn for ourselves, for that part of us that has been lost. We fantasize a dramatic enactment of our feelings, push them to the extreme, and then return to life.

The Life of Suicide

There are those, of course, who do not return, who are driven to act on their feelings in reality. In this respect, suicide is a failure of the imagination. The despair runs so deep that fantasy cannot achieve its purpose; only the act itself will do.

Psychiatrist Leslie Farber pointed up the radical difference between potential suicide and suicide fantasy when he wrote that "the awareness that it is possible to kill ourselves does not lead us to embrace suicide, any more than does the awareness that we are sinners prompt us to go forth and sin. For the man who is caught up in what I have called 'the life of suicide,' however, the possibility of being the author of his own death exercises a demonic and seductive fascination over him."

For Kirilov in Dostoevski's novel *The Possessed,* suicide is the act of will, the only antidote to fear. "I am awfully unhappy, for I am awfully afraid," he says; he can only annihilate that fear through killing himself. For a man who has lost all hope, suicide, ironically, becomes the only hope remaining. The difference between suicide fantasies and this kind of potential suicide is one of awareness.

To reject the possibility of causing one's own death, in full knowledge of its possibility, and to face instead the hard task of living with fear and of reconstructing hope, is perhaps the truly heroic aspect of living. Rollo May once wrote that he doubted "whether anyone takes his life with full seriousness until he realizes that it is entirely within his power to commit suicide," yet added that this conscious awareness is quite a different matter from "the overwhelming and persistent depression, with the self-destructive impulses unbroken by self-conscious awareness, which seems to obtain in actual suicides."

In the life of suicide, annihilation of self-awareness is the main aim; the thought of suicide becomes obsessive. And the obsession itself annihilates awareness; it is the death of intelligence and individuality, of intention and direction. It can even, however shockingly, be compared with obsessive love.

The obsession with love and the obsession with death are both a desperate and unconscious search for self-annihilating intensity when nothing else at all has meaning. Anthropologist Jules Henry observed that "life can be polarized between love and death only if there is no intensity in between; only if everything else has dropped out of life; only if there is nothing else on which to bestow meaning. . . . When life is empty, man flies from death into love; and when he cannot love he is frightened of death and so turns to love obsessively. Obsession with love and death fills the void left by the departure of significance from life, and significance is driven out of life, paradoxically, when the effort to survive becomes too much for us."

If we can face depression as a symbolic "little death" and as the process of mourning that part of us which has been lost, we are far less likely to seek self-annihilation in an obsession with death or even in death itself. But if we refuse that process out of fear or shame, we enter another kind of death—a continuing and chronic depression where the present no longer really exists, where there is and can be no future, and where suicide becomes not a matter of the imagination but of intention. The life of suicide takes over, and fantasy is rejected for fact. The fear of death is lost, so that death then becomes the lodestone of the person's life, shining beckoningly with the promise of no more awareness.

The fear with which we think about our own suicide, then, is life-preserving, and the many people who fear their own suicide fantasies are more courageous—more herioc even—than they imagine. Recognizing the possibility of suicide, they knowingly reject it and in so doing reaffirm, despite everything, a commitment to life.

The Business of Living

The flirtation with suicide may play an important role in our coming to terms with loss. In depression we feel deadened, as though part of ourselves had died. By thinking of suicide, we then create a physical metaphor for this psychic death. The idea of our own physical death, and the mourning we do imaginatively for it, becomes a dramatic means of working through the emotions of the smaller psychic death we have experienced. In imagining our own deaths, we mourn that part of ourselves that has been lost by means of mourning the loss of the whole of our life. By finally rejecting the idea of suicide, we begin to work through to an acceptance of the fact that while part of us may have died, we still live on as a whole, and the sense of self can be recovered. We begin to work through to a reaffirmation of both self and life.

The use of death imagery to reaffirm a commitment to life is a universal theme. Throughout the myths, legends, and religions of the world, we find the same story: the journey into the underworld by what Joseph Campbell called "the hero with a thousand faces," and the return from the underworld with a renewed sense of personal and universal meaning. In the traditions of the three great monotheistic religions, the desert took the place of the underworld: Moses's forty days and nights alone on Mount Sinai, Jesus's forty days and nights of being tempted by the devil in the wilderness, Mohammed's forty days and nights in the desert until he heeded his calling.

But though we can accept this encounter with death in myth or religion, we reject it in personal terms. It is hard for us to see any relationship between the hero's confrontation with death and our own personal trembling fantasies. The hero's encounter with death is valid; our own is not, even though sometimes it may be absolutely essential, as in the ability to imagine the terrible consequences of a nuclear war.

Objectively, there is no denying that we can be the authors of our own deaths, whether on a personal or a universal scale. The issue is not the possibility itself, but how we deal with it.

Hope dies much harder than we think. Although there may seem to be no immediate answer to the question "What is there to live for?" there is, somewhere within us, the conviction that there might *be* something worth living for in the future—sometimes almost a determination that there will be. The poet Gerard Manley Hopkins had this determination when he struggled with despair. Read these lines aloud and you gasp for breath with the short staccato phrases, reaching with Hopkins for the courage to endure:

> Not, I'll not, carrion comfort, Despair, not feast on
> thee;
> Not untwist—slack they may be—these last strands
> of man
> In me or, most weary, cry I can no more. I can;
> Can something, hope, wish day come, not choose
> not to be.

That reaffirmation of life is hard come by, obviously. Easier by far for many to use denial instead, especially the apparently brazen and "realistic" defense of black humor. One can understand the apparently flip cynicism of a Dorothy Parker, for example, who covered her pain by poems such as the following: "Razors pain you, Rivers are damp, Acids stain you, And drugs cause cramp. Guns aren't lawful, Nooses give, Gas smells awful, You might as well live." The same false bravado was expressed by a lawyer who passed by the open office door of a colleague and looked in; the colleague was obviously deeply depressed because it was his forty-sixth birthday. "Cheer up," said the lawyer, "you'll soon be dead."

Such approaches are attractive because the reaction to them is laughter. They pull you away from the edge with a wry cynicism that implies that there's nothing much to live for but since we're all in the same boat, what difference does it make? It is easier than searching for answers to impossible questions such as the meaning of life, and it feels more grown-up, as though with the accretion of years we also develop some kind of psychic insulation that is meant to shield us from the rough weather of existence. Such humor is often essential: stripped of illusion, we cannot always confront a stark reality directly. But if we consistently refuse to do so, we may never be able to come to terms with our own thoughts and fantasies, or with their function.

Besides acting as a dramatic form of mourning, suicide fantasies also establish a certain feeling of control. If we can control our own deaths, then we can control our own lives as well. One of the most painful feelings of depression is that of complete lack of control over one's own life. The idea of suicide can then represent the ultimate form of control—if not over the content of life, then at least over the length of it.

For this reason, both the Catholic and the Jewish faiths deliberately deny normal burial to a suicide so that others may see that it is literally beyond the bounds, even of the cemetery. The very idea of suicide is outlawed since it is seen as a usurpation of the role of God. By playing with the idea of causing one's own death, one establishes one's own individual control over both life and death; what was formerly in the hands of God is now in one's own hands. To reject suicide knowing that it is possible is a reaffirmation of faith, not in God, but in oneself and in the possibility of a future.

This sense of ultimate control can even offer a certain comfort. Martin Neufeld, a civil rights lawyer, uses the idea of suicide in this way. "There've been times when I've even planned it out carefully," he says, "thinking about the details of the will to be checked, papers to be put in order, finances settled so that there'd be as little inconvenience as possible after I was gone. And then I realize that I'm not really ready to do it yet. I mean, I know I can do it if I want to, and that's consoling in a way. It gives me an option. Then I can say, 'Well, life is disgusting right now, but I'll continue with it for a while yet, and if it's still disgusting then, then I can still do it if I want to.' That is, I keep it by as a kind of last resort, an assurance that I don't *have* to go through all this nonsense if I decide I don't want to any longer. And just knowing that seems to be enough. Then I can get on with the business of living."

9 The Obsession with Cure

*Finding out about a television program the day after it has been screened is rather like being told you just missed a great party. You tend to resent the information and would really rather not know. But on this particular morning late in 1981, there was no way I could ignore the stream of phone calls telling me about the report on depression that had been on a television news program the night before.

The first caller was a journalist. One always expects that journalists should know better, but they too are only human. "Lesley," he said, "did you see *20/20*? It's fantastic! Nobody need ever be depressed again!"

"It does sound literally fantastic," I replied.

"But they proved it, on the program," he said.

No sooner had that conversation ended than the

phone rang again. This time it was a businessman whom I had interviewed a month or so before. "They say you can have happiness injections!" he told me. "It's wonderful! I'm going to call my doctor this morning." I tried to prepare him for disappointment, but he was far too excited to listen.

The third caller was a secretary, working for a high salary in a place she despised. "It's just a matter of the right chemicals," she informed me, "there's nothing more to it. Now you can have shots against depression, just like for influenza."

I called the network and asked for a screening of the report. A time was arranged for the next afternoon. By then I was extremely curious. I knew the work on the chemical basis of depression, and knew too that while drugs developed on the basis of that work were effective in many cases of severe depression, they were of little help in mild or normal depression, and might even be contraindicated. It was also clear that the depression experienced by the people who had called me—and who kept calling through the rest of that day—was well within the range of the normal. I couldn't see how antidepressants could help them. But I did want to see how they had been led to believe that this was possible. The idea of "happiness injections," after all, was very seductive.

I settled down in a conference room the next afternoon together with one of the program's assistants. The segment was about twelve minutes long, brief even by *20/20* standards though in-depth compared to the usual news reports. It featured three severely depressed hospitalized patients and was structured like an Anacin commercial—before and after. Before antidepressants, the patients were tearful, found it hard even to speak, and were utterly miserable. After the drugs, two were lively and smiling; the third had experienced no appreciable improvement but was still on medication and hopeful—which is in itself an improvement. In all three instances, I had no idea how much time had elapsed between "before" and "after." The impression given was that the dramatic changes in the first two patients had taken place practically overnight.

As so often with television, the message was stated implicitly, not in words but through visual images: antidepressants are a miracle cure for depression. Nowhere did the narrator actually say any of the things my callers had told me, but I could see how they had jumped to those conclusions.

I found that I was getting angry at how unrealistically the piece was raising audience expectations. It seemed to me to be manipulating the universal desire for freedom from pain and encouraging people in the illusory hope that they need never be depressed again. But by the end, anger turned to amazement.

The narrator read out a list of eight questions, which were also flashed on the screen. If your reply to five or more of these questions in the last month had been "Yes," chances were you might be suffering from depression. The questions were: "Have you had a marked change in appetite or weight? Are you having difficulty sleeping? Do you notice a loss of energy? Do you have agitated or anxious feelings? Do you have a diminished interest in sex? Have you excessive feelings of guilt? Do you have difficulty concentrating? Do you have thoughts of suicide?"

Nearly all these questions were matters of judgment, not fact.

"We've had hundreds of phone calls about this report," said the assistant. "It's unbelievable. What a fantastic piece!"

"Tell me," I said, "when this piece was screened in your weekly review conference prior to screening, how did everyone here react to that questionnaire at the end?"

He laughed. "Funny you should ask that. It turned out that *we* were all depressed!"

It was hardly a surprising answer. In a high-stress atmosphere such as that of *20/20*, the staff become exhausted, nervous, anxious, and often depressed. They would be inhuman if they did not. But with that strange distancing that often afflicts news people working on "a story," nobody on the program's staff had apparently believed that they suffered from severe depression or that they needed any chemical intervention beyond the caffeine, alcohol, Valium, and other drugs commonly used by those called on to work under constant high stress.

The program aroused so much interest for one simple reason: it offered the tantalizing possibility of cure. Unwilling to tolerate depression or to come to terms with it, we insist that there must *be* a cure. It only remains then to find it. We search for it with increasing desperation and become obsessed with the very idea.

Absence-of-pain Junkies

In Aldous Huxley's *Brave New World*, everyone takes a drug called Soma, a panacea that cures all ills that humans are capable of feeling. In fact, it does away with feeling. It creates a chemical haze in which the imbibers feel no pain and experience no hurt. But neither do they have any self-reflectiveness, any conscience, or any deep emotion.

It now seems that Huxley had more foresight than even he would have cared to admit. Seduced by the hope for Soma, we have begun the search for the good life through avoidance of pain. We have become absence-of-pain junkies.

"Americans are probably the most pain-conscious people on the face of this earth," said Norman Cousins. "For years we have had it drummed into us—in print, on radio, over television, in everyday conversation—that any hint of pain is to be banished as though it were the ultimate evil." And banished with a vengeance.

In 1982, some unknown madman murdered several people in the Chicago area by placing poisoned Tylenol Extra-Strength capsules on pharmacy shelves. In each case, the person who was killed had a headache. But I could not help noticing that every time the person took not one regular-strength Tylenol for the headache but two extra-strength Tylenols. That fact made me wonder how many Americans do this, stamping out any hint of pain with far more medication than is necessary.

We long for indifference to pain. Drugs can indeed

give us this. They do not "cure" pain or treat the causes of it, but they do make it "go away" by altering our perception of it, blocking us from caring about it. I remember once taking codeine for a badly abscessed tooth, which had caused my whole cheek to swell as though I had a small apple in my mouth. It looked grotesque, but I had urgent errands to do before my appointment for surgery, and was not about to let an abscessed tooth stop me. As I was doing the errands, people looked at me in horror and sympathy and exclaimed about how much it must hurt. "It does hurt terribly," I replied, "but I feel fine"—and went floating off down the street on my codeine cloud.

Not that taking drugs to alleviate pain is anything new. Narcotics have been used throughout history for both physical and psychological pain. But the hunger for absense of pain seems to have increased in direct proportion to the growth of the pharmacopeia of pain relief. As a result, we forget how much pain we can bear if we have to.

"Unbearable" is surely one of the most overused words in the modern lexicon. It is nearly always used incorrectly, generally by people talking about pain they have suffered. If that pain had been truly unbearable, they would not have survived it to talk about it.

We can bear far more than we know, but give ourselves little chance to discover that. Instead of dealing with the conditions of our lives, we deal with the surface of them—the symptoms. Whatever causes the pain we feel is irrelevant; the only relevant thing is to make the pain go away. It is an attitude almost childlike in its naive simplicity.

A top executive working sixteen hours a day under heavy stress, for example, is quite likely to develop severe headaches. Yet the answer is not for him to reconsider the conditions of the job, but to take something for the headaches, as if the pain came from nowhere, will go back into that nowhere, and has no relation at all to reality. Instead of seeing the essentially problematic nature of day-to-day existence— its stresses and strains, tensions and hurts—the growing antipain lobby sees the symptom as the cause of pain.

This same attitude has now been transposed to depression. Whether it is called an illness (which must then have a remedy) or a problem (which must then have a solution), dealing with it has become a matter of efficiency. Get rid of the symptom (feeling depressed, or the awareness of depression), and like the magician displaying his empty hat on stage, we say that it's gone.

Like that stage magician's empty hat, however, the cure is too good to be true. It assumes that what we feel has no validity. It changes how we feel about a certain reality because it cannot change the reality itself. Thus it is basically a form of escapism. We avoid pain not by restricting our lives, but by altering our perception of it.

The development of antidepressants in the seventies has given rise to a new wave of enthusiasm in the antipain lobby. Chemicals give us a convenient "handle" on depression: they are measurable, in however small amounts, so that we can talk about physical entities instead of intangible experience. As psychiatrist Leslie Farber asked, "Is it any wonder that large numbers of sufferers of all sorts and degrees of discomfort are only too glad to fling aside the particularity, the messy concreteness, the uncertainty of meaning of their private, personal torment, and enlist in the ranks of Depression, where the only forced marching will be back and forth to the pharmacist? What have they to lose but their pains?"

Ironically, they have to lose what they once valued so much—the very awareness that was once assumed to lead automatically to mental health and happiness. But in fact to be aware is to experience both happiness *and* depression. As Farber astutely noted, chemistry may make people *feel* better, but it will not *make* them better in any sense of the word— neither better people nor better in the sense of "cured." They have merely been subjected to a solution or, rather, to a dissolution: the awareness of depression has been dissolved.

The Amine Solution

Chemical treatment of depression is based on the fact that our bodies are finely tuned to our emotions. When we are alarmed, for instance, adrenalin production increases; when we are relaxed, it decreases. Yet nobody has argued that we become alarmed *because* our bodies are producing more adrenalin; on the contrary, it is quite clear that the increased adrenalin production is a reaction to whatever experience has alarmed us. It is connected to something threatening or frightening in our environment, and our reaction to it.

In a similar way, our brain chemistry changes when we are depressed. It also changes, of course, when we are happy, anxious, or angry. Yet nobody has yet argued that we become angry because our brain chemicals have changed. Particularly in recent years, however, it has been argued that we become depressed for that reason.

Brain chemistry research began to focus on neurotransmitters, the substances that carry nerve impulses from one brain cell to the next, in the early sixties. Over two dozen have been identified so far, though there may be as many as two hundred. Two of these—the biogenic aminesserotonin and norepinephrine—seem to play a particularly important role in depression.

When someone is depressed, the level of norepinephrine, for example, often decreases. Artificially raise norepinephrine levels in the brain of a nondepressed person, meanwhile, and that person experiences increased alertness and sometimes an increased capacity for pleasure. Clearly, norepinephrine is related to feeling good and feeling bad. An antidepressant drug would thus be one that successfully manipulated the levels of norepinephrine in the brain.

Two major kinds have been developed. The first tackles the problem directly at the source, where norepinephrine is released into the central nervous system. An alkaloid called reserpine, orginally used to control high blood pressure, was found to decrease norepinephrine production, and was used successfully in treating hyperactive and manic patients. It also produced "behavioral depression" in laboratory animals; they became sluggish and developed physical symptoms similar to those of severe depression in humans. So researchers looked for a drug that would act in exactly the opposite way from reserpine. They came up with imipramine, the major drug of a series known as "tricyclics" because of their chemical structure. Imipramine speeds up the release of norepinephrine from its production center deep in the brain stem. More recent quadracyclic drugs such as iprindole also seem to increase the brain's supply of serotonin and norepinephrine in this way.

Clearly, biochemists need to think rather like chess masters, approaching problems from various angles and often solving them in an almost devious manner. Thus the second major kind of antidepressant acts in a more round-about manner than the first. It is based on an enzyme that metabolizes norepinephrine and serotonin, and inactivates them. This enzyme is called monoamine oxidase. The problem was therefore to inhibit the monoamine oxidase—in a way, to inhibit the inhibitor. The resultant antidepressant is thus called a monoamine oxidase inhibitor; it prevents monoamine oxidase from lowering the concentrations of norepinephrine or serotonin in the brain. Block the oxidase, and you unblock the biogenic amines.

These antidepressants have been a major hope for treatment of severe depression for over a decade now, and have alleviated much suffering. But their use in normal depression is still highly debatable.

When natural levels of norepinephrine decrease below a certain point, it might seem clear enough that the person in question is suffering from severe depression. But again there is the unresolved question of where one establishes that certain point, and to what degree fluctuations in norepinephrine levels are to be considered normal or abnormal. The idea of simply measuring everyone's norepinephrine levels to determine whether they are depressed (as though they did not know it) is tempting—until you realize that each individual has a different tolerance for depression, so that high chemical levels for one person may be low for the next. Even with chemicals, where we draw the line between depressed and nondepressed is still either arbitrary or a matter of judgment. As Myer Mendelson had to conclude in his textbook on depression, "the biological understanding of neurotic [mild or normal] depression is light years removed from our very imperfect but developing grasp of the biochemical events accompanying endogenous [severe] depression."

In sophisticated professional treatment, the main aim of antidepressant drugs is not to "cure" depression, as the media would have it, but to alleviate the symptoms to the point where the severely depressed person is at least amenable to psychotherapy. As one psychiatrist put it, "When we 'treat' depression we really preside over its course. We try to guard our patients from death and lesser complications, and we try to hasten the remission process." The real professionals are thus far more modest—and realistic—than the hard-sell popularizers.

Their caution is well justified. Psychiatrist Jules

Bemporad, for instance, found that antidepressants had little effect on mild depression, and that most mildly depressed people receiving them complained of unpleasant side effects: dry mouth, sedation, disorientation, and "psychomotor confusion" (when your body just will not do what you want it to do).

I discovered this to my disillusionment during my own period of deep depression in 1980. My doctor, seeing my distress, persuaded me to try Elavil, a popular antidepressant (in fact, 75 percent of all antidepressants are now prescribed not by psychiatrists but by family or general physicians). I shrugged, took the prescription, went to the pharmacy, and that night, as instructed, took one. The next morning I woke up, got out of bed, and fell down. I found I couldn't get up again. My mouth felt as though I had smoked about ten packs of cigarettes the day before. My head felt as though I had drunk about ten bottles of cheap red wine.

The phone rang. I crawled across the floor to it, picked it up, and found that I couldn't speak. Exercising what in retrospect seems great presence of mind considering the circumstances, I unplugged the phone, crawled back to bed, and slept the drug off. When I woke up late that afternoon, I went straight into the bathroom and flushed the rest of the bottle down the toilet. Sadly, I looked at myself in the bathroom mirror and came to the inevitable conclusion that I was not severely depressed.

The reason for these side effects is that antidepressants work on the somatic, physical symptoms of depression, which are far more marked when it is severe. Insomnia, anorexia, physical slowness, lack

202

of appetite, disorientation—the increasing lack of major physiological vital signs—can be treated effectively with antidepressant drugs, but in normal depression these are either absent or relatively low-key. Thus a powerful drug may be used to treat very mild symptoms.

In fact, about half of all patients receiving antidepressant drugs drop out of treatment because of the side effects, which may indicate either that these drugs are still too unpleasant for widespread use, or that these people were not suffering severe depression in the first place.

Even when it is severe, antidepressants produce only partial improvement in many patients, and a sizable number of those who improve after short-term use relapse within a year or two. So although antidepressants are often highly effective, they are far from being a miracle drug. Their use is still to some extent experimental, with psychiatrists "trying a higher dose" or "seeing if it might work better if we combine this one with another one."

The best detailed study of their effectiveness is a series of three reports by Allan Raskin, the last of which was published by the National Institute of Mental Health. He matched antidepressants against placebos—sugar-coated pills with no active ingredient. (In placebo trials, not only do the patients not know that the doctors are using placebos, but the doctors administering the drugs do not know themselves whether they are giving placebos or active drugs at any specific time. They are acting "blind" so that they will not convey to the patient their belief in the efficacy of the pills they are prescribing.)

The first study, done with severely depressed hospitalized patients, acted as "control" for the next two. Raskin simply measured the "spontaneous recovery rate" within the first year, that is, the times when recovery happened of its own accord, without connection to any kind of therapy. He found a spontaneous recovery rate of 44 percent.

The second study pooled the results of twenty-three others using antidepressant drugs and placebos in blind trials. Here, Raskin found that 46 percent of newly hospitalized acutely depressed patients improved on placebos. The antidepressants produced only slightly better results.

In the third study, Raskin found a 36 percent improvement rate with placebos, and a 44 percent improvement rate with antidepressants. Some of these patients were not severely depressed but suffering a very acute bout of what Raskin called "neurotic" or "reactive" depression. These patients responded far better to placebos than did psychotic or severely depressed patients. Sometimes, in fact, they responded better to placebos than they did to antidepressants.

"For many patients," Raskin concluded, "depression is a self-limiting illness with a high spontaneous recovery and high placebo-response rate. Neurotic depressed patients generally did as well or better in hospital with placebo as with active treatment. Neurotic patients also showed less tolerance of the adverse effects of the drugs than psychotic patients, and more were dropped because of serious side effects."

If "neurotically" depressed patients recover as well on placebos as on drugs, and even better, then why use drugs? And when? Confronted with this dilemma, some experts have argued that severe depression is a completely different syndrome from normal or mild depression. Others go so far as to suggest that whatever personal reasons elicit depression, once it reaches a certain level it "becomes biologically autonomous and consequently requires somatic therapies"—in other words, that it takes on a kind of life of its own. Yet others argue that some people have a biological disposition to severe depression, which can be altered with antidepressants. All, however, remain extremely cautious about generalizing from severe to mild depression.

Jules Bemporad, coauthor with Silvano Arieti of *Severe and Mild Depression,* which is perhaps the most exhaustive and certainly the best professional book on the subject, cautions against hospitalization for mild depression, even for acute bouts of it. "It might help in the short run," he says, "in that the individual is able to get the dependent nurturing and attention from others that he so desperately desires. However, in the long run, hospitalization would increase the depressive's resistance to doing things for himself and further hinder the needed realization that he must solve his problems by his own efforts." There is no "magical relief," he stresses. Psychotherapy is hard work, and seeking a hospital cure may even prolong or worsen mild depression.

In a society used to thinking in terms of illness and cure, such conclusions are hard to take. But the fantasy of cure and the insistence on instant relief are really only another means of self-alienation. If "it's only organic," then there is nothing one can or has to do—except go to the doctor and take the pills. In the end, antidepressants may become the treatment of choice for depression simply because they are in tune with the depression itself, reinforcing the feeling of helplessness so common to it. "There's nothing *I* can do," the depressed person can say. "It's not me, it's chemical."

The Chemical Chimera

What has been left unclear in the general reporting of biochemical advances and treatment is that biochemists are still researching the chemical correlates of depression, not the causes of it. Of course we can change how we feel through chemistry; we can take tranquilizers, cocaine, Quaaludes, aspirins, alcohol, amphetamines or marijuana, to mention only the best-known common drugs. But with none of these do we assume, as we now tend to do with antidepressants, that we are curing ourselves of how we felt before.

The question of chemical depression boils down to a chicken-and-the-egg problem: which one comes first? If we assume that chemical change does indeed precede and therefore cause depression, then the cure of depression is a simple matter: change the chemistry. But if we assume that the chemical change is only a reaction to depression (as is increased adrenalin a reaction to alarm), then chemical change is not a cause but only a symptom of depression.

Imagine, said Silvano Arieti, that a husband has a

fight with his wife. "As a consequence, he and his wife may both be very unhappy, depressed. The wife goes into the bathroom, to the cabinet, and takes a Valium. After twenty minutes, she doesn't feel depressed any more. What does that mean? It means only that this biochemical substance has prevented her organism from feeling the depression that under natural conditions she would feel. Likewise, her husband may go to a bar and have two or three martinis. But the circumstances have not changed. The fight with his wife is real. The human organism has been designed by evolution to react with depression to such a situation."

Certainly we can alter the perception of experience chemically. But have we then "cured" experience? And are we to *be* cured of experience?

To explain depression as a matter of the apparently random behavior of brain chemicals when it can be far more coherently explained as a logical reaction to life's difficulties surely stems from an overriding desire to avoid those difficulties in ostrichlike fashion instead of dealing with them.

The chemical aspect of depression thus remains the subject of much debate within the psychiatric community. Which side psychiatrists take in that debate depends less on the relatively limited facts available than on their own general outlook and beliefs about human experience and behavior. Those for whom behavior is the only relevant factor will side on the "chemistry first" faction of the debate; for them, depression is the result of chemical change. Those who have more respect for experience, like Arieti, take a different approach.

"I do not deny that a chemical event occurs in the brain when people experience depression," he wrote. "In fact, I believe that a chemical event occurs when they experience sadness. But the chemical event is an effect, and to some extent the medium, of the psychological event, with which I—as a psychiatrist, psychologist or therapist—am mainly concerned. . . . It seems plausible that the leap is not from chemistry to psychology, but from psychology to chemistry."

As Arieti makes clear, it remains a matter of opinion. There can be no definite proof on such questions. Yet it is quite clear that if someone we love dies, this is what makes us depressed, not chemical change, which occurs afterward. There is no reason to assume that it be otherwise for other forms of loss.

To look for a chemical imbalance in the brain and still pretend that everything else is fine constitutes a peculiar kind of blindness engendered by the obsession with cure. Chemistry can lessen severe depression, but it cannot prevent us getting depressed; nor should it. To imagine that it can is only another form of escapism.

Escape Routes

As though we were trapped in some Alcatraz of the mind, escape is the one great fantasy left in depression. Suicide fantasies, as we have seen, are a common form of escape. Some of the new depression therapies basically offer little more than escape from feeling. Chemistry provides an escape from the mind through antidepressants. But there are other chemical solutions too, far more widespread and far more pernicious. The flight from depression leads to sometimes desperate solutions.

Bernard Mack, for instance, nearly killed himself trying to escape it. He was hospitalized twice for heroin overdoses, and the second time it seemed doubtful that he would ever emerge alive. Now, twenty years later, he still remembers quite clearly why he was so attracted to heroin in the first place. "I thought that to be in a euphoric state in some way equaled happiness," he explains. "But it turned out to be dangerous too, because afterward there was always this crash. You go up and you come down twice as hard. And I guess I just didn't want to come down. This state of high excitement—I felt that's what living was all about. Everything else was dead by comparison. But I was wrong—it's unreal to want that to happen all the time when you're with people."

Yet unreality is seductive, especially at times when reality is just too hard. Drug experts now see the widespread use of cocaine in the American workplace as one of the major health problems of the eighties. It is also a problem of work quality, since cocaine gives you the marvelous illusion that everything you do is brilliant, even though it may be less than mediocre, if not simply bad.

Long used to block physical pain, cocaine is now used to block psychological pain as well. A temporary euphoria now offers an easy but expensive out from the problems of living and work. But the irony of cocaine use is that a vicious cycle is set in motion. Those using it need to work more in order to pay for it, and the increased work load creates more stress; the greater the stress, the more the perceived need for cocaine to alleviate it; and the more cocaine is used, the more work must be done to pay for it and therefore the greater the stress. . . . As a chronically depressed artist who had just fallen out of this cycle in sheer exhaustion mournfully remarked, "Cocaine is God's way of letting you know you're a failure."

Chemical escape has become so common that its language has spread to other forms of escape. Club Méditerranée, for instance, advertises its holidays as "the antidote to civilization," and has been tremendously successful worldwide because it has tapped into one of the most common escape fantasies of all—physical escape to an ideal place where the world can no longer "get" to us and where nothing at all is demanded of us. It is, in its way, the adult version of the child's fantasy of running away from home.

Many people cherish the idea of a certain place as a future possibility. It is not a definite goal in life, not something they will strive to achieve, but a special corner in the mind that assures them that if they ever did want to, they really could escape.

A retired publisher's assistant has nurtured the vision of a deserted beach in Maine for as long as she can remember. "It would be a small comfortable cottage," she says, "just big enough for me and nobody else. I'd spend my time reading and walking on the beach, picking up odds and ends that the sea had brought in, and I'd cook and eat when *I* wanted to and not when somebody else expected to." She would leave her husband, her children, and her grandchildren in another world, and find her peace on her own terms, far away from them all. "It's a good fantasy," she says, "a comforting one. I know I'll never do it, but just thinking that I might do, that in theory at least I have the option, just that helps me through."

A social worker who has been working "too long" with homeless people tells himself that "there's always New Zealand." Not that, as any New Zealander can tell him, there is no depression in New Zealand, but simply because he knows nothing about the country. "So far as I'm concerned, it's a place of beautiful landscapes, lakes, mountains, fresh air, where nothing ever happens, because you never read anything about it here in the news. Of course I know it's not true, except for the landscape part. Of course I know there are problems there, and depression too. But you see it's far away, almost as far away from here as I can get, away from all this. . . ." And he sweeps his arm around to indicate the dirt and poverty and misery of life in the big city for the jobless and homeless.

My own escape fantasy used to be a Greek island. In fact I even know people who carried out that very fantasy . . . for a few years. Somehow it never lasted more than that, and they returned, complaining of too many others who had adopted the same fantasy and come to the islands, "gentrifying" them and making them into small colonies of exiles. Listening to them, I gradually shifted the focus of my escape fantasy to New Zealand, for the same reason as the social worker—I knew very little about it. I even contemplated a trip there to explore it, but then realized that if I wanted to retain my fantasy, I had better not go. New Zealand would become real, and however good it might be, I would be left without my idealized escape route.

Considering how common such fantasies are, it may be surprising that so few people ever do act on their escape fantasies. Perhaps we know, without acknowledging it, that we would just pack our troubles with us if we ran away. Yet the prevalence of such fantasies does indicate awareness of one important factor: physical movement, in itself, can help deal with depression. It can break the feeling of static helplessness. We don't have to travel to deal with depression, but we do have to move.

Moving On Out

Can physical movement create psychological movement? It seems unlikely when asked that baldly, and yet many people find that when they feel stuck psychologically, physical movement helps them on through.

Poet May Sarton, for example, found that she could pull up weeds—a lovely metaphor for clearing out depression. She "worked out anguish in a garden" and "learned to clear myself as I cleared a pasture." Setting to furiously with scythe and hoe at an overgrown garden can be a very satisfying day's work, but for those who do not have gardens, let alone overgrown ones, all kinds of other physical activities do just as well. My own favorites have been, at various times, mountain climbing, karate, running, or dancing. The metaphor of such activities is clear: ascending, punching, moving, clearing, bouncing—in all of them, physical activity translates into psychological terms. A healthy tiredness overtakes the body: not the tiredness of lassitude and apathy, but the satisfying one of having used one's energy to the full. Dissatisfied exhaustion becomes a satisfied tiredness.

Of course this process can be partially explained as biochemistry. During physical activity, the brain produces more endorphins, which are the body's "natural opiates." But the effect of physical movement on depression lasts longer than any temporary increase in endorphin level. It sets up a different way of relating to the world, as though the movement itself had raised one up from the heaviness of depression, slicing through it as though through a thick fog.

"Getting into shape" thus becomes an effort of redefinition, of rebuilding and reconstructing the sense of self through movement. The awareness of a healthily tired body is very different from the awareness of an exhausted one. Sometimes, it can be exhausting just to sit and do nothing.

As analyst Edrita Fried explained it, we have to move about as psychological beings to stay in shape, "much as the body must be exercised and put through diverse uses of muscles if it is to stay resilient and healthy." Physical and psychological mobility are firmly connected. Even so small a thing as standing upright, as Fried noted, can establish the path from passivity to activeness.

Strenuous forms of activity may not even be needed. Yoga, meditation, and other relatively passive methods such as the Alexander technique can work as effectively as running or swimming. The choice of movement is more a matter of personality, it seems, than of necessity. The essential seems to be the attention to physical sensation and the awareness of movement, stillness, form, and shape.

Music too can establish this bridge to activeness. For years, I have picked out certain pieces that I think of as "movement music"—not necessarily music to move to, as in dancing, but music that seems to me to have an urgency or spirit that speaks of psychological movement. It is music that is hard to ignore and that demands response. It changes from time to time, as I change. At the time of writing, for instance, it focuses on Beethoven's Eighth Symphony and on the music of Greek composer Mikis Theodorakis, though I am perfectly aware that by the time these words are read, these preferences may well be different. Meanwhile, they have seen me through many a bad time.

All these forms of movement segue into psychological movement, breaking the static quality of depression. Movement on any level, it seems, creates movement on others. Expending physical energy can create psychological energy, and perhaps here the stress should be less on physical movement as such than on physical awareness—the sensation of aliveness and of the potential for movement, which frees one from that oppressive feeling of being trapped.

But still, physical awareness remains only a means of dealing with depression, a useful thing to know but not something that will allow of any greater insight into ourselves or why we get depressed. If we are really to come to terms with depression, we must go further, looking first for tolerance and then for understanding of how we feel and why. For most people, psychotherapy offers a safe framework in which to do this. Ideally, it provides an accepting environment in which to examine themselves and their lives and to rediscover a sense of possibility and vitality. But even when it *is* ideal, therapy offers no easy escape or cure, not even at its best—in fact, especially at its best.

The Real Role of Psychotherapy

Few therapists today—whether psychiatrists, psychologists, analysts, or social workers—seem to have either the humor or the realism to appreciate Freud's remark that he cured the miseries of the neurotic only to open him up to the normal miseries of life.

Freud remains one of the most overquoted and underread shapers of twentieth-century thought. It is often assumed that the idea of psychological cure began with him, but in fact he never believed that such a thing as cure existed in psychotherapy. He acknowledged that the idea of cure is basic to medicine, but he never saw analysis as a "medicine for the mind." Instead, he fought long and hard against the whole idea of permitting only medical doctors to become analysts. "Psychoanalysis is not a medical speciality," he insisted. "I do not see how one can resist recognizing this. Psychoanalysis is a part of psychology."

He lost the battle in the United States, where the desire to scientize analysis and give it the respectability of medicine means that most analysts have spent the major part of their training in medicine, concentrating on the pathological instead of the normal. Where Freud used the image of illness and its treatment only as a metaphor, the vast school of psychoanalysis established on the basis of his work chose to see it as objective fact.

Bruno Bettelheim, in his impassioned demonstration of how Freud's emphasis on the soul was misunderstood and even mistranslated into pseudomedical terms, argued that this whole attitude has led to unreal expectations of analysis: "It is expected that anyone undergoing psychoanalysis will achieve tangible results—the kind of results the physician achieves for the body—rather than a deeper understanding of himself and greater control of his life."

The illusion of cure is still deeply embedded in the whole idea of psychotherapy. But in fact good therapy offers no magic. It offers only hard work. If relief is all that one seeks, the pharmacist can supply it better than the therapist.

Yet I do not believe that those seeking therapy are as naive in their expectations as Bettelheim imagines. There is a widespread desire for relief, true, but just as widespread a desire for understanding. And the very fact of seeking therapy can itself be an act of some courage.

Men in particular think of going into therapy as an act of weakness. The implied acknowledgment of lack of control is particularly hard for them since it clashes with the masculine stereotype. To overcome this and acknowledge the need for help is itself an important step forward. As psychiatrist M. Scott Peck has pointed out, "Even at the outset of therapy, and contrary to the stereotypical image, people in therapy are basically much stronger and much healthier than average."

By the very fact of entering therapy, a person acknowledges his or her loss of the illusion of control. This demands courage, but it also carries its own reward. By acknowledging loss, one begins to work through it. Without this acknowledgment, there remain only the fear and shame of being depressed.

Above all, a good therapist can act as a bulwark against the fear of one's own feelings, offering support, warmth, and sympathy—all the things we might also find in a close friend or relative if friends and relatives were only more tolerant of their own and others' depression. Particularly at the outset, therapy also offers a great deal of reassurance—perhaps because people still have the illusion that the therapist, as an external agent, can do the work for them. Of course no therapist can, but by the time the person in therapy discovers this, they have also discovered their own courage, and are ready to do the work themselves.

The "secret" of therapy, insofar as there is one, lies not so much with the therapist as with the person seeking it and their reasons for doing so. Too many, as we have seen, still come seeking cure, as though their lives were infected in some way and needed to be made healthy. They come to therapy in the hope of finding some magic charm to take away the pain—and on occasion may even be deceived by those therapists who claim to possess what they are looking for. But others come after deeper thought. They come disillusioned, knowing and acknowledging a feeling of helplessness. The question then is whether they want illusion to be restored, or whether they are willing to undertake the task of facing life in all its imperfections and searching out courage and faith in themselves.

What then is the role of the therapist? First, a good therapist will offer not cure but courage. He or she can give understanding, challenge, and support—a safe framework in which to identify and work through loss. Second, a good therapist will relieve the obsession with cure, encouraging patients to look at their feelings rather than block them. Third, and I think most important, a good therapist will urge patients to go beyond their immediate sense of loss to the core of what they consider important in their lives, helping them to examine their values and to follow through from the experience of depression to a reconstruction of meaning and relevance.

Compared to all those claims of cure and eternal happiness, this is hard work. But you cannot cure life. Good therapists will not deceive themselves about this—or you. Aware of the vicissitudes of life and of human values and emotions, they will not describe the kind of depression you probably experience as sick or irrational or unnecessary. On the contrary, perhaps the most important thing they will do for you is to respect you and your feelings.

10   The Road of Transcendence

"Most people shrink when in despair or depression, but it can also be used constructively, as an opportunity. The despair can then act upon the person like the flood in Genesis: it can clear away the vast debris—the false answers, false buoys, superficial principles—and leave the way open for new possibilities. That is, for new freedom."

This is analyst Rollo May talking about the constructive possibilities of despair. He makes it sound weird and wonderful. But it is obviously also extremely painful. It seems as though only a particularly gifted but tortured few could possibly break through on such a level.

We almost expect creative people to go into the depths of despair. Not for them the garden-variety depression most of us know, but the utter depths, where they may plumb some realm of experience fortunately closed to most of us. We tend to accept their despair as part of the "artistic personality." Some of the more cynical among us might even suspect that they are playing it up for effect, behaving according to their own stereotyped image of how an "artist" should feel.

If they drink a lot, take drugs a lot, "act out" in ways that we would not tolerate for ourselves—why, all this, we think, is part and parcel of being a creative person. We can accept their depression more easily than our own, perhaps because we hold creative endeavor in such respect.

Yet this same dramatically exaggerated depression is just as noticeable in the lives of those from whom we least expect it—the saints and the mystics, the very people we hold up as models of how we should and could be. Reading their writings and accounts of their lives, I was struck by how similar their cycles of depression were to the creative ones. In both instances, depression seemed to be the prologue to a breakthrough, whether of creation or revelation. It seemed to be not so much an antagonist in their lives as an essential stage in their work or thought. It occurred to me that it might even be more friend than enemy, since it was the means through which they struggled to some kind of transcendence.

I think it worthwhile to look at this unusual role of depression not because I think we should aim to be like these extraordinary people—in fact I think we should not—but because their experience dramatizes the positive aspect of depression. While their depression seems deeper and more agonizing than ours, their joys seem to be commensurately higher, even reaching into ecstasy. By pushing themselves to the limits of existence and emotion, they have discovered and even depend upon depression as a constructive factor.

The Pain of Creativity

"We who dwell in the heart of solitude are always the victims of self-doubt," wrote Thomas Wolfe in his essay "God's Lonely Man." "Forever and forever in our loneliness, shameful feelings of inferiority will rise up suddenly to overwhelm us in a poisonous flood of horror, disbelief and desolation, to sicken and corrupt our health and confidence, to spread pollution at the very root of strong exultant joy. And the eternal paradox of it is that if a man is to know the triumphant labor of creation, he must for long periods resign himself to loneliness, and suffer loneliness to rob him of the health, the confidence, the belief and joy which are essential to creative work."

It may be a sudden fit of "frozen horror," he wrote, or something "so vague as to be a hideous weather of the soul." Whichever, "all of the joy and singing of the day goes out like an extinguished candle, hope seems to me lost forever, and every trust that I have ever found and known seems false."

The truth is that I envy Wolfe for being so used to "all the joy and singing of the day" in the first place. Even while I sympathize with the darkness of his depression, I am seduced by the way he describes coming out of it: "Suddenly, one day, for no apparent reason, his faith and his belief in life will come back to him in a tidal flood. It will rise up in him with a jubilant and invincible power, bursting a window in the world's great wall and restoring everything to shapes of deathless brightness. Made miraculously whole and secure in himself, he will plunge once more into the triumphant labor of creation."

And plunge Wolfe did. This was the man once heard walking through the night streets of Brooklyn chanting, "I wrote ten thousand words today!" the man who brought his manuscripts to his publishers by the cartonful, and who wrote as nonwriters imagine writers writing—the words flowing from his pen. The sheer energy of the man informed his depression as much as it informed his creativity. Both, it seems, were experienced with an intensity beyond the bounds for most of us.

This intensity sprang from a basic element in Wolfe's life: "The lonely man, who is also the tragic man, is invariably the man who loves life dearly— which is to say, the joyful man. . . . The one condition implies the other, and makes it necessary." If he wanted to keep writing, he realized, he would have to stick with the doubt, despair, and confusion that he called loneliness, since out of that shattering feeling of complete helplessness sprang the urge to create new forms and images and to discover unique ways of expressing experience.

Critic Leon Edel maintains that all great writers create out of depression, or what Benjamin Rush called "tristimania." I am not sure if all do, but I do know that most do, and I know too that one resists this piece of information. It doesn't quite make sense at the first hearing; it seems an infuriating paradox, in fact. After all, we think of creativity as the wellspring of life, while depression can feel like a little death. How then can depression be integral to creativity?

If normal life contains within it the element of depression as a reaction to loss, all the more so the abnormal life of creativity. Most writers know the stifling feeling of emptiness and exhaustion that comes when they have finished a work, and the accompanying conviction that there can never again be anything worth writing about or that they will never again be able to write as well as they have in the past.

Partly this is postpartum, and partly, ironically, it is the down that comes after success. Something new has been created and given independent existence in the world. The question "What now?" becomes a haunting presence, and depression is the struggle through to discovering the answer to that question.

Creativity is based on relinquishing accepted and fixed assumptions, on tearing oneself away from what already exists in order to discover or create what does not yet exist. Of its very nature, it demands a fresh outlook, a fresh perception. If you feel that everything has already been said, of course there is nothing left to say. But the excitement of finding a new way to say it, or even something altogether new to say, is familiar to all good writers.

The creative process is thus a repeated pattern of lost and found. It may be that one needs a certain personality for this—a particularly high tolerance for depression, perhaps. Or it may be that those who write are forced into tolerating depression because it is built into their work. I doubt if it can ever be established which way it goes. But certainly nearly every writer is familiar with emptiness. Creation, after all, is based on emptiness, on the initial existence of nothingness.

One creates from emptiness and returns to it afterward in order to find the space for the next creation to grow. Depression becomes the nothingness in which "something" begins.

Virginia Woolf suffered severe depression on and off until she finally killed herself, but she believed that this depression was essential to her work. It was partly mystical, she claimed. "Something happens in my mind. I refuse to go on registering impressions. It shuts itself up. I become a chrysalis. I lie quite torpid, often with acute physical pain. . . . Then suddenly something springs."

Kafka suffered depression for months on end, and his sense of helplessness guided his work, which is full of a feeling of gloomy suffocation and futile repetition. Keats wrote that "Full many a dreary hour have I past, My brain bewildered, and my mind o'ercast With heaviness." And Goethe, at the end of his life, tragically declared that his life had been "nothing but pain and burden, and I can affirm that during the whole of my seventy-five years, I have not had four weeks of genuine well-being. It is but the perpetual rolling of a rock that must be raised up again forever."

The question "Is it really worth it?" is a valid one. It seems almost sacrilegious just to ask it, since it implies a judgment on practically the whole of our literature. I doubt that there can be any definitive answer. To say "yes" means that we selfishly accept the product of suffering and ignore the suffering itself; to say "no" means that there would be no product. But what is really striking is that the people involved never seem to have asked that question. Some vital urge kept them writing and creating, made them accept the emptiness and the depression that were part of their work and their lives. Creativity has a price, and they were willing to pay it. That is our good fortune, and in the end, it is impossible for us to even try to judge whether for them it was fortune or misfortune. They were committed to a life of struggle.

The Joyous Melancholics

"Our way of saying you have to be mentally healthy is that you have to be up *and* down," says Adin Steinsalz, waving his pipe in illustration as we talk in his Jerusalem home about Judaism. Although he is an orthodox rabbi, he is far from the classical image. His red hair trails in wistful curls over his high forehead, his pockets are full of leftover bits of tobacco, and his eyes twinkle with enjoyment as he plays with ideas that he knows will sound shocking to his listener. Originally a physicist and mathematician, he is now, in his midforties, a widely respected authority on Talmud and Cabala.

His whole philosophy stands in stark contrast to the bliss and contentment offered by Far Eastern traditions. The traditional Jewish way is one of struggle and curiosity, he emphasizes. It is one of always reaching further and of never being satisfied:

"A second-century Talmudic description of a *tzaddik* [Judaism's closest equivalent to a holy man] is that 'the righteous have no rest, not in this world and not in the next,' " he explains. "This is a definition not of the wicked, but of the righteous, because they have so much to do that they can never be restful. You can see it in all the biblical heroes: none of them are restful, none of them without blame. There are no rosy pictures in the Bible. They are all in struggle, and this is what makes them great. There's a medieval saying that if you knew the Lord, you'd *be* Him. So trying to know Him is like trying to catch the horizon; the more you try, the more you understand the distance, yet the more you yearn for it."

But surely, I object, such awareness of the impossibility of it all could lead to despair.

"So long as you're struggling, quarreling," he replies, "there can't be despair. Despair is one of the supreme sins, because a despairing person ceases to struggle. That makes despair the ultimate defeat; it is death. It has a feeling of completeness to it, closely connected to smugness. The despairing person makes no attempt to move from the point he is at—no attempt to change himself or the world—and this completeness is a mark of dying. Dying is completion."

He leans back to think a moment, arms behind his head, then goes on:

"A famous rabbi was once talking of what a great, full life his grandfather led. A follower pointed out that his grandfather had died very young. 'What do you think?' replied the rabbi. 'People are clothes to be washed out and dried and used again? No, they finish what they have to do and then depart!'

"The idea is that if you have nothing more to do and have fulfilled what you had to do, that is the end of the story. The content of the story is not in the length of it, but in the process of it. The whole idea of Judaism is process: incessant oscillation, up and down, heavenward and earthward. Like breath, this is life. And the purpose is not in the being up or the being down; it is in the movement, which creates life. So sometimes the only way to move someone out of despair is to make him bitter, to force him to feel, to suffer, and thus to struggle. One of the beautiful things about the exodus from Egypt is that before it the children of Israel 'embittered their lives.' Before they did that, they accepted the conditions of exile; by embittering their lives, they could not stand it anymore. And this is the beginning of any kind of deliverance. If you are satisfied—things may not be so great, but they're tolerable, let's say—then you stay in one place, and there's no movement, no life."

For all of us, emotional and psychological variation are not luxuries or self-indulgence, but essential if we are to retain a sense of vitality. The Jewish mystical movement even made a virtue out of necessity, its masters becoming joyous melancholics in their struggle with God. Many of the charismatic Hassids experienced dramatic bouts of acute depression. Some, such as the seventeenth-century Hassidic predecessor, Shabbatai Zevi, went even further, into manic-depressive psychosis, in the manic phases of which he assumed the title of the Messiah.

Others yearned for the euphoria of mania but battled mainly with depression. Rab Itzikl Horowitz, the Holy Seer of Lublin, was one of these. Prevented by a fellow rabbi from throwing himself over a cliff when he was still a young man, he complained that the world was too flat. It lacked fire and passion, he explained, and this leads to indifference and resignation—in other words, to death. What is worse than suffering? he asked his students later. The answer was indifference. And what worse than despair? Resignation, meaning the inability to *be* moved, to let oneself go, or to let one's imagination catch fire.

The Baal Shem-Tov—the founding father of the Hassidic movement—once called depression the greatest sin because it keeps a person from doing anything good or indeed from doing anything at all. But he also saw that it could be an essential part of the experience of joy. The sin was not in *being* depressed, he said, but in *staying* depressed. Depression itself could be used to come closer to God.

The Hassids developed the old Cabalistic idea of "descent for the sake of ascent." If a thought occurs that takes you away from God, they said, you must go down in your mind and pursue it, find the "spark of holiness" in it, and bring it back up to God. In modern times, this would translate as rechanneling the energy so that it feeds upward instead of feeding on itself with diminishing returns. The principle is the same: transform the energy, "raise it up."

Knowing how to get his students' attention, the Baal Shem-Tov used the example of lust. Originally, he said, lust came from the palace of divine love. You have to be able to see its origin and to understand

229

that it has merely undergone a transformation. That being so, it can then be transformed back into love.

Another melancholy Hassid, Nahman of Bratslav, saw depression as a constant aspect of every personality. He used the parable of a melancholy man standing to the side and watching a circle of Hassids dancing. Even when you are happy, he said, the constant melancholy aspect of you stands to the side and watches as you dance. So you must grab hold of it, pull it into the circle, and transform it so that it becomes part of the circle. Why this need for force? Because if you leave it standing there to the side, it will destroy happiness. True happiness is impossible, Nahman maintained, if part of you is standing back looking. That part, the melancholy part, must be brought into the circle, or it will drag you out of it.

"The main thing is that one must always struggle with all one's strength to be joyous always," he said. "It is the nature of man to be drawn into melancholy and sadness, because of the things that happen to him; every man is filled with sorrows." To deal with these sorrows, Nahman even made a rule of "breaking the heart." For one hour a day, in solitary prayer and meditation, you should purposely be miserable. This hour was intended to act as a catharsis, working out the grief and depression that might otherwise be the undercurrent to the whole day. In it, Nahman ruled that you should talk aloud to God, vocalizing despair and thus allowing it an outlet. He thus came up with an early form of talking cure or psychotherapy, with God as therapist.

Nahman remained well versed with depression until the end of his life. He had no rules for avoiding depression—that was a given of human life—but only for dealing with it. And he seemed to realize that the mystic pursuit involved perhaps more and deeper depression than the normal. "You see in me a great beautiful tree with wonderful branches," he once told his followers, "but the roots of that tree are lying in Hell." It was a warning, alerting them to the curse and the blessing of the mystical search, one that had long been known in Christian mysticism as the dark night of the soul.

The Dark Night of the Soul

The delving down and inward that seems to be an essential prelude to mystic experience is a particularly agonizing form of depression. It exists in all the mystic traditions of the world, either as directly expressed helplessness and hopelessness or as a symbolic crisis or night journey—visiting the underworld like Orpheus, being cast down like Joseph at the bottom of a well, being buried as Jesus was, or swallowed alive like Jonah.

Saint John of the Cross saw it as a state of "passive purification." The intensity of the pain of it was so great that he called it deathlike. Aware of the existence of another level of perception—direct revelation—yet unable to reach it, he mourned his own helplessness. "I live, yet no true life I know," he wrote—the prototypical experience of every person in depression, haunted by the feeling that though one is physically alive, there must be more to life than this.

"The soul is conscious of a profound emptiness in itself," wrote John, "a cruel destitution of the three kinds of goods, natural, temporal, and spiritual, which are ordained for comfort. It sees itself in the midst of the opposite evils, miserable imperfections, dryness and emptiness of the understanding, and abandonment of the spirit in darkness." It sounds familiar enough to most of us, but for mystics, it had a purpose: it was the prelude to revelation, the price of ecstasy.

This is how Evelyn Underhill described the dark night in her classic volume *Mysticism*: it is "the intervening period of chaos between the breakup of an old state of equilibrium and the establishment of the new. The self, in its necessary movement towards higher levels of reality, loses and leaves behind certain elements of its world, long loved but now outgrown. . . . The exhaustion and ruin of the illuminated consciousness is the signal for inward movement of the self towards other centers; the feeling of deprivation and inadequacy which comes from the loss of that consciousness is an indirect stimulus to new growth. The self is being pushed into a new world where it does not feel at home, has not yet reached the point at which it enters into conscious possession of its second or adult life. . . . Psychologically, then, the Dark Night is due to the double fact of the exhaustion of an old state, and the growth towards a new state of consciousness."

The dark night is thus a kind of growing pain in what Underhill called "the organic process of the self's attainment of the Absolute," and "great mystics have known instinctively how to turn these psychic disturbances to spiritual profit."

Those of us far less concerned with absolutes and more involved with worldly troubles than with spiritual profit can still understand. These mystics were basically acting out a universal human experience on a more dramatic and presumably more exalted level. They entered the dark night with conscious purpose where most of us enter it against our will. While few of us experience or perhaps even want mystic revelation, nearly all of us know times of "metaphysical disquiet," or what a friend of mine once called "a bad case of the existentials." The mystics had no monopoly on darkness.

When the dark night was allowed its sway, the reward was considerable: uncertainty could be transformed into certitude, confusion into clarity, hesitation and fear into courage and determination. The very fact of facing it seemed to strengthen and maintain the spirit. Out of the depths came the heights of experience.

One of the most lucid accounts of this struggle is Tolstoy's *My Confession,* which is almost a diary of the prolonged dark night he suffered in his early fifties. "I felt that something had broken within me on which my life had always rested," he wrote, "that I had nothing left to hold on to, and that morally my life had stopped. . . . I did not know what I wanted. I was afraid of life; I was driven to leave it; and in spite of that I still hoped for something from it."

This overwhelming crisis came at a time when everything seemed to be going perfectly in his life. Yet the questions insinuated themselves: "What will be the outcome of what I do today? Of what I shall do tomorrow? What will be the outcome of all my life? Why should I live? Why should I do anything? Is there in life any purpose which the inevitable death which awaits me does not undo and destroy? These questions are the simplest in the world. From the stupid child to the wisest old man, they are in the soul of every human being. Without an answer to them, it is impossible, as I experienced, for life to go on. . . ."

Suddenly ordinary life, which had indulged Tolstoy very nicely up to that point, seemed "meaningless asburdity." Suicide seemed the only logical course. "Yet whilst my intellect was working, something else in me was working too, and kept me from the deed—a consciousness of life, as I may call it, which was like a force that obliged my mind to fix itself in another direction and draw me out of my situation of despair. . . . I can call this by no other name than that of a thirst for God."

The very awareness of "something else" came to consciousness in depression, through a deep disenchantment with life. Writing about Tolstoy's conversion in *The Varieties of Religious Experience,* William James saw the depression as "getting his soul in order" and as "the escape from falsehoods into what were for him ways of truth." When disillusionment has gone this far, said James, "there is seldom a *restitutio ad integrum.* One has tasted of the fruit of the tree, and the happiness of Eden never comes again. The happiness that comes, when any does come . . . is not the simple ignorance of ill, but something far more complex, including natural evil as one of its elements, but finding natural evil no such stumbling block and terror because it now sees it swallowed up in supernatural good. The process is one of redemption, not of mere reversion to natural health, and the sufferer, when saved, is saved by what seems to him a second birth, a deeper kind of conscious being than he could enjoy before."

Through his depression, maintained James, Tolstoy had found "a stimulus, an excitement, a faith, a force that reinfuses the positive willingness to live."

It took Tolstoy two years to acknowledge and accept his need for faith. "Since mankind has existed," he then wrote, "wherever life has been, there has also been the faith that gave the possibility of living. Faith is the sense of life, that sense by virtue of which man does not destroy himself, but continues to live on. It is the force by which we live. If man did not believe that he must live for something, he would not live at all."

For Tolstoy, this meant rejecting the life of the upperclass intellectual for what he saw as the simple peasant life—no matter what the cost to those close to him. The accepted picture of his conversion and his later life is an attractive one, even a seductive one, since it leaves out as much as it includes. In fact Tolstoy's resolution of his crisis was never as firm as his admirers believed. Yet since we all yearn for that perfect resolution, he became something of a guru to a whole generation of socialists, philosophers, and theologians. "Though not many of us can imitate Tolstoy," William James wrote admiringly, "not having enough, perhaps, of the aboriginal human marrow in our bones, most of us may feel at least as if it might be better for us if we could."

The minute someone talks about "aboriginal marrow" with such admiration, however, we suspect an intellectual romanticization of the primitive. Another romantic intellectual who longed for that quality and who created it superbly in his novels was Nikos Kazantzakis, the poet of vitality whose passionate mysticism informs all his writing, from *Zorba the Greek* through *The Temptation of Christ* to his magnificent *Odyssey*. The picture he created was immensely attractive and yet almost heroic in its proportions. We would all love to be Zorba, yet even those who have tried it have eventually been forced to acknowledge the difference between a fictional ideal and the possibilities inherent in reality.

Nevertheless, it remains a fine inspiration. "God is the most resplendent face of despair, the most resplendent face of hope," wrote Kazantzakis. Depression was not only a form of exile from vitality; it was also the struggle back to the full experience and richness of life. This struggle demands extraordinary determination and even defiance, as demonstrated by Kazantzakis's story of the man who climbs a mountain to find the face of God: when he reaches the peak and finds only sheer rock, rather than despair he takes out a chisel and begins to carve a face into the rock. . . . Whether he carves in anger or frustration, in determination or defiance, does not really matter—so long as he carves, acts, moves, protests, and continues in the attempt to change the unchangeable.

All these figures—novelists, mystics, rebels, and

iconoclasts—live on a plane of intensity that seems admirable from a distance but exhausting from too close. We admire them, find inspiration in them, and even hold them up as heroes. We can identify the basic principles underlying their lives and apply them to our own. Yet we do not really think of them as role models. Most of us—I think wisely—are looking for something else for ourselves. Transcendence and redemption are too much; we want something calmer, something more lasting, something more mature.

11 The Making of Maturity

When I first conceived of writing this book, I naively hoped that in the course of working on it, I would work all depression out of me forever. Despite all common sense, I still retained more than a glimmer of faith in the infamous key-to-eternal-happiness, thinking that if I only knew more, the key would be mine, velvet cushion and all.

The more I worked, however, the more it became clear that something very different was happening. I realized quickly enough that pat solutions and magic keys would get us nowhere; they were chimeras, products of our own hopes and illusions. But it took time to let go of easy hope, however false, and to realize something far more promising: that once the overlay of depression could be conquered and the fear of facing it overcome, depression itself was not at all the ogre that has been drawn for us.

Reading through much of the popular material available on depression, I sometimes wonder what image the writers have of their readers. Often, it seems that they see us as easily frightened children, terrified of the dark. On the one hand, they increase that terror by telling us all the awful things that can happen in the dark; on the other, they soothe us by telling us that we only imagine all these things, and they're not real. Then they feed us the bedtime stories they think we want to hear, and for a short time we too can become the supermen and superwomen of psychomyth—never depressed, eternally happy, and perfect.

But these new bedtime stories for adults are far from relaxing. They make us demand more and more of ourselves; we can never do or be enough. Perfection can always be stretched to a further limit. And instead of a mature acceptance of limits, we are led to believe that there are none.

Now we can have "life extension," as though living longer were a virtue in itself, unrelated to the quality of that life; we can use biofeedback to accustom ourselves to hitherto unbearable amounts of stress and tension; we can run, leap, swim, and ride faster than ever before, but though the four-minute mile is already history, we break more and more records to what seems to be less and less purpose. Even vitality is fast developing into a hyper jitteriness where all is movement, and we lose contact with the still center of our selves, spinning out into social space as though we could "find ourselves" in the fleeting refractions of others' eyes.

In all this frantic reaching for perfection and happiness, there is little time left for the pains and perils of being "merely" human. And so inevitably, behind all the glitz and the glitter, there is a growing sense of dissatisfaction in the new psychokingdom. More and more people feel betrayed by the promise of too much. When the promise fails to materialize, because it can't, they are left impatient and disappointed with their own imperfection.

The brilliant colors of the sunsets painted for us give way to night, as all sunsets must, and depression is there to pull us back to the center, warning of inner emptiness and loss. When this happens, we might welcome it instead of feeling disappointment and fear, for it acts as the balance to the psychofads—the antidote to hubris, and a vital reminder of our fallibility and vulnerability. Like it or not, it keeps us human.

"There is no sun without shadow," Albert Camus once wrote, "and it is essential to know the night." In an age that seems to want to banish the night altogether, such knowledge is all the more important.

The Courage to Be

If you are overwhelmed by the fear of depression, flight seems the obvious solution. But the paradox is that facing it, which seems at first glance to be the harder way, is in fact the easier. Suffering once accepted loses its edge; the terror of it lessens, and what remains is generally far more manageable than we had imagined. When we come face to face with it, the ogre comes down to human size.

"Allow the demon that wishes, to scream, protest and swear, all freedom to have its way," pronounced Alan Watts in buddhistic manner, and "as often as not it does not need it, for the very act of granting it the freedom is in itself a relief."

Granting ourselves this freedom is a matter of learning faith in ourselves—faith in our own normalcy, in the validity of what we feel, in our rationality and humanity. But as many an analysand has discovered, knowing something does not necessarily make it easier to deal with. Indeed, it may make matters more difficult. One needs courage to tolerate awareness; only the ignorant need none.

Paul Tillich called it "the courage to be"—the courage to accept the fact that perfect control and satisfaction are neither possible nor desirable, and that our humanity and vitality are rooted in our remaining imperfect and vulnerable. Accepting this means far more than simply nodding one's head and saying, "Yes, this is true." It involves living with that knowledge emotionally as well as intellectually. It is one thing to accept depression when you are not depressed, and quite another when you are. This is the time when intellectual knowledge must become knowledge of the heart, measured not by range or scope but by depth.

"If suffering alone taught, all the world would be wise, since everyone suffers," wrote Anne Morrow Lindbergh. "To suffering must be added mourning, understanding, patience, love, openness, and the willingness to remain vulnerable." These are the conditions within which we can work through loss and change in a constructive manner, gaining in maturity. By allowing ourselves these qualities, we regain a sense of momentum, of purpose and movement in our lives.

Far more of us are capable of this than we have so far supposed. We nearly all have greater reserves of courage than we give ourselves credit for, but call on them far too seldom. By seeking external cures and attributing our feelings to misperceptions or chemicals or hormones, we forgo our own courage and ability. For lack of use, our courage will atrophy. Some of us may then face a self-fulfilling prophecy and find that it has died for lack of belief in its existence.

When we do find it, we may even surprise ourselves, like someone finding a forgotten treasure in the attic. This is how one woman in her late thirties felt when, encouraged by a wise therapist, she determined to face her depression. "I'm not as frightened of it as I used to be," she now says. "I used to get really terrified, so that the important thing was to stop feeling it and just *do* something, anything, so that I wouldn't feel. The therapy made me realize that it wasn't going to kill me, and that if I stuck with it I'd come out the other end. Which I did."

She still looks somewhat surprised that this should be so. "I remember the first time I allowed myself to go with it, not to fight it. . . . And it ended! And since I *did* go with it and didn't fight it and it *did* end, now I can face it. Now I know I can handle it.

"It's not that I'm more or less vulnerable to it than before, but I've simply accepted it as something that periodically happens. It's no longer an ogre. I've always seen it as such a weakness, a failing on my part, that I'd panic and do anything to squash that feeling. Now I don't do that. I sit down and think about it, accepting that it will be with me for a while, and I find it acts like a recouping of energy. It's a time of really taking deep breaths and thinking about what's happened."

Encouraged to struggle through the overlay to the essence of her depression, she found a relative calm, a still emptiness rather than a fearful void. Here, the patterns of loss in her life became clear; she could mourn them, and then move on.

Others may take a more compromising route. One middle-aged man finds that the best way for him, for the moment at least, "is to keep a kind of split personality about it. Part of me lets it happen. But another part stands aside and establishes limits for how far I'm going to let it go. It's a compromise that seems to work. You see, it's not just a matter of being depressed, but of being aware of what is happening. Once you have that awareness, once you know what's happening to you, then you gain some control over it. And once you have that measure of control, you don't feel like such a fool for being a grown man and depressed."

There was no mysterious alchemy at work here, no secret technique. Rather, the struggle against the self had ceased, and the energy previously used to fight off awareness could now be put to more constructive use, creating greater insight and understanding.

In the calm then created, there is one basic question that we should all ask ourselves: *What has been lost?*

If we can sit quietly and ask this one question, reaching over the range of possible loss from tangible to intangible, material to symbolic, it seems that we can always pinpoint it. And once that has been done, we can then mourn it properly and effectively.

It seems a small enough question, yet asking it can effect a radical change in the way we feel about depression. What was irrational becomes rational; what seemed absurd becomes an appropriate response; what seemed a waste of time becomes a valuable space within which to reconstruct meaning and purpose.

We can do this work alone or with the help of a friend or a therapist. Either way, we quickly reach the focal point of the depression. The depression itself then becomes meaningful. We stop feeling foolish; we recoup energy. And we do this not in fear, panic, or frustrated flight, but in calm and mature acceptance of ourselves.

The Imp of Imperfection

There is no perfect solution to depression, nor should there be. And odd as this may sound at first statement, we should be glad of that. It keeps us human.

Some cultures—older and more aware of hubris than our own—have known this for centuries. Antique Oriental carpets have a small flaw purposely woven into them by their Muslim makers because perfection, they say, belongs only to God. Orthodox Jews still leave a small patch unpainted in a freshly painted room because to be perfect is not of this world.

We all long for perfection. We yearn to be contented creatures, pleased with ourselves and our lot. Yet to be too content is dangerous—more dangerous than discontent. The longing for perfect contentment may be understandable—it would mean an end to struggle and striving, to uncertainty and doubt—but its achievement would be deadening. A state of entropy would be created, and that would mean the end of our world.

Entropy is a state of balance—a perfect equilibrium in which no movement at all is required. Biologically, it means an inactive or static condition, and in biology it leads to death. Natural species are in a constant state of movement, of evolution, and if there is no evolution, life comes to an end.

Psychologically, it means basically the same thing. Philosopher Miguel de Unamuno once played at admiring the word "entropy"—"a scientific and most rationalist word, a pretty word" he called it—but "for a soul avid for life, it is the closest thing to nothingness that can be imagined." Arguing passionately for what he called "the tragic sense of life," Unamuno advocated insecurity and uncertainty as the foundation of moral and ethical behavior.

But I see nothing at all tragic in this. In fact, I see it as the essence of vitality. In a presumably perfect world, there would be no depression, no suffering, no pain, not even any death. But this brave new world would be lifeless. It would be static and pointless, full of a hypnotically dull and relentless sameness. If we all had perfect bodies and perfect minds, the joy of individual difference and mutual discovery would disappear. We would know exactly what to expect, as we do of machines, for only machines can be perfect.

If all were perfect and we were fully content, there would be no need to move, no point in moving. Entropy would take over. There would be an end to all desire, since if all is ideal, there can be nothing left to be desired. But the end of struggle and the end of desire is also the state of death. It is the antithesis of everything that keeps us alive, both physically and psychologically.

Imperfection keeps us thinking, feeling, moving. Where perfection is a deadening state of entropy, imperfection is aliveness, vital and productive. As John Passmore wrote in *The Perfectibility of Man,* what people achieve "will be a consequence of their remaining anxious, passionate, discontented human beings."

One might then ask, "But who wants to be anxious and discontented?" It is the wrong question. We would do better to ask, "Who could be anything *but* anxious and discontented?" A narcissist could, certainly, or a very young and fortunate child, or a dogmatic and fanatical believer. They would have no doubts and no problems, no deep pain and no awareness of loss. But no sensitive and alive person can ever feel this on a permanent basis. They would forfeit too much.

Certainly we can prize perfection as an ideal state, and enjoy to the fullest those moments, perhaps even days, when the ideal reaches fulfillment. But to expect constant perfection and contentment is unreal. We must be prepared to mourn its passing and our consequent return to a more problematic reality. Instead of striving to prolong what cannot, by its nature, last long, we should strive for a mature acceptance of life's imperfection and even an appreciation of it.

The Color of Life

A party, a ball game, a candlelit dinner—the smallest as well as the biggest of events can produce marvelous moments of sheer euphoria. In a good movie, for instance, you may become completely oblivious to yourself and the circumstances of your own life, totally caught up in excitement, fear, or enchantment, or all three together. But such moments when we feel "taken out of ourselves" are by their nature ephemeral; they cannot be prolonged. Euphoria will not make for a satisfying life. Vitality will.

We not only wish to live; we wish to experience our own aliveness. We want to *feel* alive. But vitality reaches beyond happiness to the varied texture of life itself. It is the dynamic of life, the energy behind experience, the flow of movement essential to that feeling of aliveness.

Erich Fromm once described happiness as "our touching the rock bottom of reality . . . the discovery of our self and our oneness with others as well as our difference from them . . . a state of intense inner activity and the experience of the increasing vital energy which occurs in productive relations to the world and to ourselves."

What he was really describing was not happiness but vitality. The key elements of his description—the rock bottom of reality, the discovery of self, the intense inner activity—are also the hallmarks of depression, which reflects the indomitable human need for meaning, for relevance, and for a sense of place and purpose. But this is a Januslike need, both beautiful and ugly. Neither every minute nor every day can be meaningful. If it were, we would be so burdened with meaning that we would be completely overwhelmed by it. We need those times when we can forget ourselves, when we can create, assent to, and enjoy illusion, and allow ourselves a temporary suspension of judgment. We need laughter and play, foolishness and even triviality, but not to the exclusion of all else. The balance of awareness and illusion, of seriousness and play, can only be found through the experience of both, not through flight from the one into a desperate pursuit of the other. Each enriches the other and gives the other a deeper dimension.

This is surely the excitement of life: the conflict, the continual struggle, the oscillation between light and dark, up and down, heaviness and lightness. Vitality is contained in the movement between naked reality and playful fantasy. It is the meeting place of experience and reflection, awareness and illusion, stillness and movement, loss and finding, sorrow and joy. And if we are to remain active vital human beings, we must retain the ability to be both happy *and* depressed.

Both happiness and depression are fueled by the same source: the capacity to feel, to allow ourselves emotion, and to experience the full range of life. This is vitality. Far from being a waste of time, as so many people still insist, depression is as integral a part of human experience as is happiness. The normal course of life includes both joy and sorrow, and all the vast gray area in between.

Too many people still refuse to accept this. It is as

though they had divided their lives into black and white, and then decided that only the white is acceptable. Bewildered by the huge range of shades of gray, they choose to ignore the fact that gray exists at all. They live only for one extreme of experience. By so doing, they not only void depression of any meaningful content, they also void it of purpose. Unable to evade it, because they are only human, they block its vital function—the absorption of loss and change, and the establishing of a renewed basis on which to exist in the world. They make it into the very meaningless agony that they most fear.

Sadder still, they cut themselves off from the full color and experience of life, and thus from vitality itself. Of course there are times when we agree with the poet W. H. Auden when he wrote that "ordinary human unhappiness is the natural color of life." But it seems to me that we should strive instead for the constructive maturity advocated by Freud, for whom life was the full range of colors, from light to dark. "There can be no question of an antithesis between an optimistic and a pessimistic theory of life," he wrote. "Only the simultaneous working together and against each other of the primordial drives, Eros and the death drive, can explain the colorfulness of life, never the one or the other all by itself."

This is what we need—an appreciation of the colorfulness of life, and the pain and the delight of a complete palette. Depression too is part of the color of life, a vital dimension of being human.

Selected Bibliography

AKISKAL, H. S., and W. T. McKINNEY. "Overview of Recent Research in Depression," *Archives of General Psychiatry.* Vol. 32 (1975).

ALDRIN, EDWIN E. *Return to Earth.* New York, 1973.

ALLOY, L., and L. ABRAMSON. "Judgment of Contingency in Depressed and Non-depressed Students: Sadder but Wiser?" *Journal of Experimental Psychology, General.* Vol. 108 (1979).

ALVAREZ, A. *Life After Marriage.* New York, 1982.

ANTHONY, E. JAMES. In *Depression and Human Existence.* Edited by E. James Anthony and Therese Benedek. New York, 1975.

ARENDT, HANNAH. *On Revolution.* New York, 1963.

ARIETI, SILVANO. *The Intrapsychic Self.* New York, 1967.

_____ . In *Severe and Mild Depression: The Psychotherapeutic Approach,* by Silvano Arieti and Jules Bemporad. New York, 1978.

_____ . Interview in *Psychology Today.* April, 1979.

ARISTOTLE. *Problemata.* Cambridge, Mass., 1936–7.

BALINT, MICHAEL. "The Paranoid and Depressive Syndromes," *Primary Love and Psychoanalytic Technique.* New York, 1953.

BECK, AARON T. "An Inventory for Measuring Depression," *Archives of General Psychiatry.* Vol. 4 (1961).

_____ . *Depression: Causes and Treatment.* Philadelphia, 1972.

BECKER, ERNEST. *The Birth and Death of Meaning: A Perspective in Psychiatry and Anthropology.* New York, 1962.

_____ . *Revolution in Psychiatry: The New Understanding of Man.* New York, 1964.

_____ . *The Denial of Death.* New York, 1973.

BELL, QUENTIN. *Virginia Woolf: A Biography.* London, 1972.

BEMPORAD, JULES. In *Severe and Mild Depression: The Psychother-*

apeutic Approach, by Silvano Arieti and Jules Bemporad. New York, 1978.

BENEDEK, THERESE. In *Depression and Human Existence.* Edited by E. James Anthony and Therese Benedek. New York, 1975.

BETTELHEIM, BRUNO. *Freud and Man's Soul.* New York, 1983.

BIBRING, ERNEST. "The Mechanism of Depression," *Affective Disorders.* Edited by Phyllis Greenacre. New York, 1953.

BLATT, S.J., et al. "Experiences of Depression in Normal Young Adults," *Journal of Abnormal Psychology.* August, 1976.

BONIME, WALTER. "The Psychodynamics of Neurotic Depression," *Journal of the American Academy of Psychoanalysis.* Vol. 4 (1975).

BOWLBY, JOHN. *Loss: Sadness and Depression.* Vol. III, *Attachment and Loss.* London, 1980.

BOYD, J., and M. WEISSMAN. "The Epidemiology of Affective Disorders: A Reexamination and Future Directions," *Archives of General Psychiatry.* September, 1981.

_____ , M. WEISSMAN, W. D. THOMPSON and J. K. MYERS. "Screening for Depression in a Community Sample; Understanding the Discrepancies Between Depression Symptoms and Diagnostic Scales," *Archives of General Psychiatry.* October, 1982.

BRADBURN, N. M., and D. C. CAPLOVITZ. *Reports on Happiness.* Chicago, 1965.

BROVERMAN, I., et al. "Sex Role Stereotypes and Clinical Judgments of Mental Health," *Journal of Consulting and Clinical Psychology.* January, 1970.

BROWN, GEORGE W., and TIRRIL HARRIS. *Social Origins of Depression.* London, 1978.

BURTON, ROBERT. *The Anatomy of Melancholy.* New York, 1927 (originally 1621).

CAMUS, ALBERT. *The Myth of Sisyphus.* New York, 1955.

_____ . *Lyrical and Critical Essays.* New York, 1967.

CAVAFY, C. P. *The Complete Poems of Cavafy.* Translated by Rae Dalven. New York, 1976.

COOPER, DAVID. In *Reason and Violence,* by R. D. Laing and D. G. Cooper. London, 1964.

COSTELLO, CHARLES. *Anxiety and Depression.* Montreal, 1976.

COYNE, JAMES C. "Depression and the Response of Others," *Journal of Abnormal Psychology.* Vol. 85 (1976).

Diagnostic and Statistical Manual of Mental Disorders, 3rd ed., American Psychiatric Association. Washington, 1980.

ECKARDT, MARIANNE HORNEY. "Life as a Juggling Act: Our Concepts of 'Normal' Development—Myth or Reality?" *American Journal of Psychoanalysis.* Vol. 35 (1975).

EDEL, LEON. *Stuff of Sleep and Dreams: Experiments in Literary Psychology.* New York, 1982.

ELIOT, T. S. *The Complete Poems and Plays.* New York, 1952.

FARBER, LESLIE H. *Lying, Despair, Jealousy, Envy, Sex, Suicide, Drugs and the Good Life.* New York, 1976.

———. "Merchandizing Depression," *Psychology Today.* April, 1979.

FLACH, FREDERIC F. *The Secret Strength of Depression.* New York, 1974.

FOUCAULT, MICHEL. *Madness and Civilization.* New York, 1965.

FREUD, SIGMUND. *Thoughts for the Times on War and Death,* 1915. Vol. 14, *Complete Psychological Works of Sigmund Freud.* London, 1957.

———. *Mourning and Melancholia,* 1917. Vol. 14, *Complete Works.*

———. *Postscript to the Question of Lay Analysis,* 1927. Vol. 20, *Complete Works.*

FRIED, EDRITA. *The Courage to Change.* New York, 1981.

FRIEDMAN, R. J. and M. M. KATZ, eds. *The Psychology of Depression: Contemporary Theory and Research.* New York, 1974.

FROMM, ERICH. *The Sane Society.* New York, 1955.

———. *The Heart of Man.* New York, 1964.

———. *The Anatomy of Human Destructiveness.* New York, 1973.

GAYLIN, WILLARD, ed. *The Meaning of Despair.* New York, 1968.

———. *Feelings.* New York, 1979.

GOLDBERG, HERB. *The Hazards of Being Male.* New York, 1976.

GOVE, WALTER. "The Relationship Between Sex Roles, Marital Status and Mental Illness," *Social Forces.* September, 1972.

GREEN, ARTHUR. *Tormented Master: A Life of Rabbi Nahman of Bratslav.* University, Alabama, 1979.

GREENE, GRAHAM. *The End of the Affair.* London, 1951.

GREENSON, RALPH. "On Boredom," *Journal of the American Psychoanalytic Association.* January, 1953.

GUARDINI, ROMAN. *The Focus of Freedom.* Baltimore, 1966.

HAMMEN, C. L., with C. A. PADESKY. "Sex Differences in the Expression of Depressive Responses," *Journal of Abnormal Psychology.* Vol. 86 (1977).

———, with S. D. PETERS. "Differential Responses to Male and Female Depressive Reactions," *Journal of Consulting and Clinical Psychology.* Vol. 45 (1977).

———, with S. D. PETERS. "Interpersonal Consequences of Depression," *Journal of Abnormal Psychology.* Vol. 87 (1978).

——— (C. A. PADESKY and C. L. HAMMEN). "Sex Differences in Depressive Symptom Expression and Help-seeking Among College Students," *Sex Roles.* Vol. 7 (1981).

HARTMANN, HEINZ. *Essays on Ego Psychology.* New York, 1964.

Selected Bibliography

HAZLETON, LESLEY. "The Joyful Struggle of Adin Steinsalz," *Quest/80*. July, 1980.

HENRY, JULES. *Jungle People*. New York, 1941.

HESSE, HERMANN. *Steppenwolf*. New York, 1963.

HOPKINS, G. M. *Poems of Gerard Manley Hopkins*. Oxford, 1930.

HUXLEY, ALDOUS. *Brave New World*. New York, 1946.

INGLEBY, DAVID. "Understanding 'Mental Illness,' " *Critical Psychiatry*. Edited by David Ingleby. New York, 1980.

JAHODA, MARIE (Marie Lazarsfeld). *Current Concepts of Positive Mental Health*. New York, 1958.

JAMES, WILLIAM. *The Varieties of Religious Experience*. New York, 1958 (originally 1890).

JONES, ERNEST. *Sigmund Freud: Life and Work*. London, 1953.

JONES, HOWARD MUMFORD. *The Pursuit of Happiness*. Harvard, 1953.

KANT, IMMANUEL. *Observations on the Sense of the Beautiful and the Sublime*. Berkeley, 1960 (originally 1766).

KAUFMAN, WALTER. *Nietzsche: Philosopher, Psychologist, Anti-Christ*. Princeton, 1950.

KIERKEGAARD, SØREN. *The Concept of Dread*. Princeton, 1957 (originally 1844).

_____ . *Fear and Trembling* and *The Sickness unto Death*. Princeton, 1941 (originally 1843 and 1849).

KLEINKE, C. L., et al. "Sex Differences in Coping with Depression," *Sex Roles*. Vol. 8 (1982).

KLERMAN, GERALD, et al. "Treatment of Depression by Drugs and Psychotherapy," *American Journal of Psychiatry*. Vol. 131 (1974).

KLINE, N. In *Manic Illness*. Edited by Baron Shopsin. New York, 1979.

KOVEL, JOEL. "The American Mental Health Industry," *Critical Psychiatry*. Edited by David Ingleby. New York, 1980.

_____ . *The Age of Desire*. New York, 1982.

LAING, R. D. *The Politics of Experience*. London, 1967.

_____ . "The Obvious," *The Dialetics of Liberation*. Edited by David Cooper. London, 1968.

LASCH, CHRISTOPHER. *The Culture of Narcissism*. New York, 1978.

LEWIS, C. S. *A Grief Observed*. London, 1961.

LIFTON, ROBERT JAY. *The Broken Connection*. New York, 1979.

_____ and RICHARD FALK. *Indefensible Weapons*. New York, 1982.

MARCEL, GABRIEL. *The Mystery of Being*. Vol. 2, *Faith and Reality*. London, 1951.

_____ . *The Philosophy of Existentialism*. Secaucus, N.J., 1977.

MARRIS, PETER. *Loss and Change*. London, 1974.

MASLOW, ABRAHAM. "The Need to Know and the Fear of Knowing," *Journal of General Psychology.* Vol. 68 (1963).

———. "Neurosis as a Failure of Personal Growth," *Humanitas.* Vol. 3 (1967).

MAY, ROLLO. "Contributions of Existential Psychotherapy," *Existence: A New Dimension in Psychiatry and Psychology.* Edited by R. May, E. Angel, and H. Ellenberger. New York, 1958.

———. *Love and Will.* New York, 1969.

———. *Man's Search for Himself.* New York, 1953.

———. *Freedom and Destiny.* New York, 1981.

MENDELSON, MYER. *Psychoanalytic Concepts of Depression.* New York, 1974.

National Institute of Mental Health. *Report on the Collaborative Program on the Psychobiology of Depression.* Washington, 1980.

NURNBERG, H. G. "Narcissistic Personality Disorder," *Weekly Psychiatry Update Series.* F. Flach, ed., Vol. III, No. 18. Princeton, 1980.

OATES, JOYCE CAROL. " 'Why is Your Writing so Violent?' " The New York *Times Book Review.* March 29, 1981.

ORTEGA Y GASSET, JOSÉ. *The Revolt of the Masses.* New York, 1957.

PASSMORE, JOHN. *The Perfectibility of Man.* London, 1970.

PAVESE, CESARE. *The Business of Living.* London, 1961.

PECK, M. SCOTT. *The Road Less Traveled.* New York, 1978.

PRANGE, ARTHUR J. "Antidepressants," Vol. V, *The American Handbook of Psychiatry.* Edited by Silvano Arieti. New York, 1974.

RASKIN, ALLEN. "A Guide for Drug Use in Depressive Disorders," *American Journal of Psychiatry.* Vol. 131 (1974).

RICOEUR, PAUL. *Dread and Philosophy.* Yale, 1970.

———. *Freedom and Nature.* Evanston, Ill., 1966.

———. "Psychiatry and Moral Values," Vol. I, *The American Handbook of Psychiatry.* Edited by Silvano Arieti. New York, 1974.

ROIPHE, ANNE. "A Writer Looks at the Void," *International Journal of Psychoanalysis.* Vol. 35 (1975).

ROSZAK, THEODORE. "In Search of the Miraculous," *Harper's.* January, 1981.

SANDLER, J. and W. G. JOFFE. "Notes on Childhood Depression," *International Journal of Psychoanalysis.* Vol. 46 (1965).

SCARF, MAGGIE. *Unfinished Business: Pressure Points in the Lives of Women.* New York, 1980.

SCHOPENHAUER, A. "On Death" and "On the Vanity and Suffering of Life," *The World as Will and Idea,* Vol. III. New York, 1961.

SLATER, PHILIP. *The Pursuit of Loneliness.* Boston, 1976.

TILLICH, PAUL. *The Courage to Be.* Yale, 1952.

Selected Bibliography

DE TOCQUEVILLE, A. *Democracy in America*, Vol. II. New York, 1956.

TOLSTOY, LEO. *My Confession*. London, 1889.

UNAMUNO, MIGUEL DE. *The Tragic Sense of Life*. New York, 1954.

UNDERHILL, EVELYN. *Mysticism*. New York, 1955.

VAN KAAM, ADRIAN. In *The Goals of Psychotherapy*. Edited by A. R. Mahrer. New York, 1967.

WATTS, ALAN. *The Meaning of Happiness*. Stanford, 1953.

WEISSMAN, MYRNA, et al. "Treatment Effects on the Social Adjustment of Depressed Patients," *Archives of General Psychiatry*. Vol. 30 (1974).

_____. "Drugs and Psychotherapy in Depression Revisited," *Psychopharmacology Bulletin*. Vol. II (1975).

_____ and GERALD L. KLERMAN. "Sex Differences and the Epidemiology of Depression," *Archives of General Psychiatry*. Vol. 34 (1977).

WIESEL, ELIE. *Four Hassidic Masters and Their Struggle with Melancholy*. Terre Haute, Ind., 1978.

WILLIAMS, TENNESSEE. "On a Streetcar Named Success," the *New York Times*. November 30, 1947.

WOLFE, THOMAS. "God's Lonely Man," *The Hills Beyond*. New York, 1941.

WOOLF, VIRGINIA. *The Waves*. New York, 1931.

ZETZEL, ELIZABETH R. "Depression and the Incapacity to Bear It," *International Journal of Psychoanalysis*. Vol. 41 (1960).

ZILBERGELD, B. *The Shrinking of America: Myths of Psychological Change*. Boston, 1983.

Index

About the Author

LESLEY HAZLETON is an English-born psychologist and journalist now living in New York. She received her M.A. in psychology from Hebrew University in Jerusalem. Her work has appeared in *Harper's Magazine, The Nation, New York Times Magazine, Quest,* and *Vanity Fair.* She is the author of ISRAELI WOMEN: THE REALITY BEHIND THE MYTHS and WHERE MOUNTAINS ROAR: A PERSONAL REPORT FROM THE SINAI AND NEGEV DESERT.